Immigrant Experiences

IMMIGRANT EXPERIENCES

*Why Immigrants Come to the United States
and What They Find When They Get Here*

WALTER A. EWING

ROWMAN & LITTLEFIELD
Lanham • Boulder • New York • London

Published by Rowman & Littlefield
A wholly owned subsidiary of The Rowman & Littlefield Publishing Group, Inc.
4501 Forbes Boulevard, Suite 200, Lanham, Maryland 20706
www.rowman.com

Unit A, Whitacre Mews, 26-34 Stannary Street, London SE11 4AB

British Library Cataloguing in Publication Information Is Available

Library of Congress Cataloging-in-Publication Data Is Available

ISBN 978-1-5381-0050-9 (cloth: alk. paper)
ISBN 978-1-5381-0051-6 (electronic)

∞™ The paper used in this publication meets the minimum requirements of American National Standard for Information Sciences—Permanence of Paper for Printed Library Materials, ANSI/NISO Z39.48-1992.

CONTENTS

Introduction

It's not easy to leave the country in which you were born and raised. It's home. But sometimes you don't have much of a choice. You may find yourself forced into the position of a refugee—fleeing the violence of a military invasion, civil war, gang war, or government persecution. Perhaps conditions aren't quite that dire, but you find yourself in a losing battle to stay above the poverty line in a country where most people are poor; so you take your chances in another nation with more plentiful jobs and higher wages than you can find at home. If you're one of the luckier migrants of the world, you live a relatively comfortable life in your home country, but want to pursue bigger and better opportunities in a nation that occupies a more privileged place in the global economy. And whether you're rich or poor, you may simply want to be with family members who have already moved abroad.

Regardless of why people choose to cross international borders, not all intend to say "goodbye" to their homes forever. Many plan to go back after a few years of working or running a business or going to school abroad, thereby saving the money or acquiring the skills they need to go back home with brighter prospects than when they left. Some follow through with this plan, while some put down roots in their new home and stay for the rest of their lives. And there are those who want to stay in their adopted homeland for good, but are kicked out because they broke a law or violated an immigration regulation. This is often the case for immigrants who are undocumented; that is, those who couldn't find a legal way of migrating to their destination, but who migrated anyway because they felt that there was no viable alternative.

Just as variable as the reasons people leave their home countries are the receptions they receive when they get where they wanted to go. Even within a single destination country, the reactions of native-born citizens to the presence of immigrants can vary widely from region to region, from community to community. Some people give immigrants the benefit of the doubt and actually get to know them, while others automatically view them with hatred and suspicion—sentiments that are usually fed by uninformed stereotypes about what it means to be a "foreigner." The same group of immigrants might be welcomed in some communities, and met by angry mobs in others.

Regardless of what the native-born population thinks about immigrants, the economies of the nations to which most immigrants travel derive many benefits from their presence. Immigrants represent new workers, ranging from low-tech to high-tech. Immigrants are also new consumers, taxpayers, and entrepreneurs. In communities that find themselves in decline for whatever reason, with native-born residents either dying out or moving out, immigration can be a life-saving transfusion. In the longer term, immigrants literally give birth to new generations of native-born citizens—just as they always have—and a large percentage of natives today are only a few generations removed from their immigrant forebearers. Even so, today's immigrants are not always welcomed by the grandchildren and great-grandchildren of yesterday's immigrants.

Not all of these themes capture the realities of immigrant life in every country. But they do describe well the lives of immigrants in the United States, both past and present. In the late eighteen hundreds and early nineteen hundreds, immigrants comprised anywhere from 13 percent to 15 percent of the U.S. population and came mainly from Europe.[1] Debates raged over whether or not these immigrants were stealing jobs, committing crimes, and refusing to learn English. Fast forward to today, when the immigrant share of the population again stands at around 13 percent (although immigrants now come predominantly from Latin America and Asia), and the same debates are raging about a new generation of immigrants.[2] Some of the virulent anti-immigrant activists now on the political scene had grandparents who arrived during that last period of large-scale immigration—and who were no doubt reviled by the anti-immigrant activists of that era. It is historical repetition at its worst. It is also socially self-destructive,

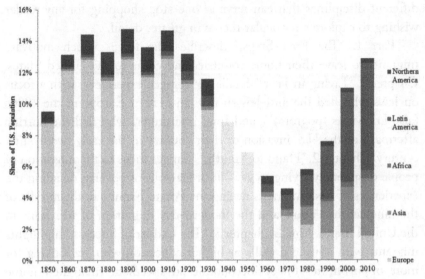

Foreign-Born Share of U.S. Population by World Region of Birth, 1850–2010
SOURCES: CAMPBELL GIBSON & KAY JUNG, HISTORICAL CENSUS STATISTICS ON THE FOREIGN-
BORN POPULATION OF THE UNITED STATES: 1850–2000, U.S. CENSUS BUREAU, FEBRUARY 2006;
2010 AMERICAN COMMUNITY SURVEY.

given that, in addition to the 13 percent of the population that was born somewhere else, another 12 percent were born here, but have at least one immigrant parent.[3] What that means is that fully one-quarter of the U.S. population has a very direct and visceral connection to immigration in some form or another.

CAPTURING COMPLEXITY
There is no one immigrant experience. There are many experiences of immigration depending on where you start out, where you're heading, and where you finally end up. This book attempts to capture the complexity of these experiences in a systematic, straightforward manner, drawing upon the research of academics, but—hopefully—writing in a more accessible style. The book is divided into three parts, and each part contains three chapters. Some material is occasionally repeated in different chapters in order to make each chapter self-contained and easier to read. And each chapter draws heavily from just a few, primarily academic sources from

different disciplines that can serve as one-stop shopping for any reader wishing to explore a particular theme in greater detail.

Part 1, "The First Steps," describes the forces which motivate migrants to leave their home countries and come to the United States. Chapter 1, "Living in Fear," details the refugee experience, with a focus on Jews who fled the anti-Jewish riots in eastern Europe in the 1880s (also known as "pogroms"), and Iraqi interpreters who fled the horrific aftermath of the U.S. invasion of their country in the early twenty-first century. Chapter 2, "Hand to Mouth," changes focus to the migration of people desperately trying to get out or stay out of poverty, detailing the experiences of Irish migrants fleeing the Potato Famine in the middle of the nineteenth century, and the modern-day migration of Mexicans to the United States. Finally, chapter 3, "The Ladder of Success," highlights migrants with advanced skills or higher education who are looking for more opportunities for socioeconomic advancement than their home countries provide. For instance, many German immigrants of the 1850s and contemporary migrants from India came here with highly specialized skills in hand, in search of new chances for upward mobility.

Part 2, "Homecomings," describes the initial receptions which immigrants receive upon arriving in the United States. Chapter 4, "Pieces of Paper," shines a light on the many obstacles which undocumented immigrants encounter as they try to navigate the unfamiliar terrain of a new country without benefit of the immigration "papers" (documents) which the federal government will not grant them. This was the scenario confronting undocumented Chinese migrants making their way across the U.S.-Mexico border at the end of the nineteenth century, as well as contemporary Mexican migrants crossing the same border. Chapter 5, "Fearing the Unknown" describes the range of hate-filled nativist responses to immigrants, especially the ire directed at Italian immigrants arriving in the United States in the 1880s and into the 1920s, and the hostility confronting many present-day Mexican immigrants. And the last chapter in part 2, chapter 6, "Warmer Welcomes," highlights the welcoming responses which some immigrants have received. In the nineteenth century, this welcome often came from previous immigrants who encouraged their countrymen to join them on the other side of the ocean. Today, formal "welcoming initiatives" have been designed in cities like New York which not only try to make immigrants feel welcome, but to facilitate their integration into U.S. society.

Part 3, "The New Ordinary," looks at the long-term impact of immigration on U.S. society, and the impact that U.S. society has on immigrants and their descendants. Chapter 7, "The Bottom Line," details the impact of immigration on the U.S. economy, as well as the limited upward mobility experienced by many immigrants themselves. In the nineteenth century, for instance, Irish immigrants played a major role in building cities such as Boston and New York, while Chinese and Mexican workers built the railroads of the West. Beginning in the late twentieth century, Latin American and Asian immigrants fueled the growth of enormous swaths of both high-tech and low-tech industries, in the process filling labor-force shortfalls left by the aging of the native-born populace. Chapter 8, "Generation Gaps," delves into the ways in which the children of immigrants differ from their parents. As an example, the children of Mexican immigrants attain both higher levels of education and higher rates of criminality as they gradually transform into Americans. Finally, chapter 9, "New Identities," deals with the ways in which immigrants (and their children and grandchildren) change the cultural mainstream of the United States, even as the mainstream culture changes them. The cultural impact of immigrant communities can be felt in all sorts of ways, ranging from the popularity of bagels to the popularity of hip-hop.

This is a lot of ground to cover. But no real understanding of immigration can be distilled into the sound bites so often used by politicians and political commentators. It is a topic that touches upon every aspect of U.S. society, both past and present, and intersects with virtually every field of human knowledge, from economics and political science to anthropology and linguistics.

Who Am I?

My knowledge of immigration is derived primarily from nearly two decades spent conducting immigration policy analysis and research in the nonprofit sector in Washington, DC. For fifteen years I have been a researcher at the American Immigration Council, a pro-immigrant advocacy and legal organization. During my time at the Council, I have studied and written about the impact of immigration on the U.S. economy and U.S. workers, the relationship (or lack thereof) between immigration and crime, the ineffectiveness and inefficiency of U.S. border-enforcement policies, and the faulty logic of the faux research disseminated by anti-immigrant organizations. My writing on these topics has been designed to convey the complexities of immigration to readers who are educated, but who are not immigration experts. Prior to my time at the Council, I spent two years as an immigration policy analyst for the U.S. Conference of Catholic Bishops and two years as a program director at the U.S. Committee for Immigrants and Refugees. It was in these positions that I first wet my feet in matters related to U.S. immigration policy.

Prior to my work on immigration, I spent many years making my way through a PhD program in cultural anthropology at the City University of New York (CUNY) Graduate Center. Although my academic exposure to the scholarly literature on immigration was relatively minor during this time, my anthropological education turned out to be very relevant. My topical area of specialty was international development and my geographical area was Latin America. Given that most immigrants to the United States come from Latin American nations, learning about their histories and traditions proved useful in my later career as an immigration researcher. More important, though, was learning to approach the world with an anthropological perspective. Immigration knows no bounds. It is a historical, social, cultural, political, economic, and transnational phenomenon which cannot be fully understood without a holistic perspective. The hallmark of cultural anthropology is precisely that kind of holistic perspective. I have tried to provide a perspective in this book that is as holistic as possible, while also striving to keep the number of pages at a manageable level.

All of the opinions expressed in this book are my own and do not necessarily reflect the views of any individual or organization for whom or for which I have ever worked.

PART I
THE FIRST STEPS

CHAPTER ONE

Living in Fear

SOME PEOPLE DO NOT WILLINGLY LEAVE THEIR HOMELANDS BEHIND. Confronted by persecution, war, or some other form of collective violence, they seek safe haven in another country. If they make their way to the United States and successfully request protection, they are granted asylum. If they successfully request protection while still outside of the United States, they become refugees. Either way, these are individuals who face the prospect of death, imprisonment, or torture if they remain in—or return to—their home countries.[1] Their journeys are frequently terrifying and often involve split-second decisions rather than carefully planned itineraries. Today, refugees are flowing out of Syria, Afghanistan, Somalia, South Sudan, Sudan, Democratic Republic of the Congo, Central African Republic, Myanmar, Iraq, and Eritrea. By mid-2015 there were 15.1 million refugees worldwide—the highest number recorded in twenty years. The countries to which they flee (such as the United States) sometimes have narrow definitions of who is worthy of protection, which leaves many people out of luck who are truly in need. It is well worth remembering that there were also an estimated thirty-four million internally displaced persons as of 2014; people who fled violence, but who never crossed an international border in the process, so they are not refugees per se.[2]

NEW WAYS OF KILLING

Sadly, there have long been nations engulfed in conflicts or ruled by dictators that generate an exodus of men, women, and children seeking refuge. Throughout both the nineteenth and twentieth centuries, millions of people have crossed international borders in the process of running for their lives to escape armed conflicts.[3] A particularly hideous twentieth century innovation when it came to the killing of civilians—and generating refugee flows—was ethnic cleansing. Although massacres of noncombatants were nothing new in the history of warfare, the genocidal slaughter of people on the basis of ethnicity, race, or religion as a means of achieving some imagined state of national purity was definitely new. And despite formidable progress around the world in raising awareness of fundamental human rights, ethnic cleansing continues to resurface as a tool of demagogues searching for scapegoats to blame for the social and economic problems of their nation.[4]

The earliest case of what could properly be called ethnic cleansing was the Turkish government's killing of Armenians during World War I (1914–1918). But the most infamous case in history came during World War II (1937–1945) with the Holocaust, in which Germany's Nazi government sought to create a nation that was Aryan (which is to say Nordic and Germanic, not to mention fascist) by systematically killing millions of Jews, Roma (gypsies), homosexuals, disabled persons, and communists. The Nazis built concentration camps in which gas chambers and crematoriums were specially constructed to facilitate mass murder on an unprecedented scale.[5] The international backlash against the enormity and brutality of the Holocaust culminated in the war crimes tribunal in Nuremberg, the formal conceptualization of certain depraved acts as crimes against humanity, and the adoption of the Universal Declaration of Human Rights by the newly formed United Nations in 1948. Nevertheless, ethnic cleansing campaigns have proven to be a recurring phenomenon. Over the decades, from Indonesia to Cambodia to Rwanda, members of particular social groups have found themselves targeted for extermination—ostensibly in the interest of the nation. Needless to say, no matter where or when it occurs, ethnic cleansing has generated large numbers of refugees seeking to escape death.[6]

Although the United States is often romantically portrayed as home to the world's refugees, starting with the Pilgrims and their quest for religious freedom, the truth is a bit more complicated. For instance, as anthropologist David W. Haines points out, the Jamestown settlers did indeed come to this land seeking freedom—but it became a very particular form of economic freedom which was built on the backs of African slaves. In the nineteenth century, the U.S. government actively made refugees out of the Native Americans who inhabited the southeastern portion of the country; driving them westward in order to steal their land while killing a great many in the process.[7]

The twentieth century offers other examples of either hostility or ambivalence towards refugees on the part of the United States. In 1939, a ship full of German Jews fleeing the Nazi regime tried to land in the United States, but was refused and ultimately went back to Europe— even though many on board had secured pledges of financial support from individuals or private organizations. The reason was simple, if distasteful: there was a strong strain of anti-Semitism running through U.S. society, and many politicians did not want to bring any more Jews onto U.S. soil than there already were. Of course, this stance became a bit more untenable at the end of World War II, when the horrors of the Holocaust became undeniable, but—before then—the United States more or less abandoned European Jews to whatever fate they might meet under the Nazis.[8]

The resettlement of Holocaust survivors in the United States once the war ended did not signify that the doors were now thrown open wide for all refugees in need. In fact, when President Truman admitted a relatively small number of "displaced persons" into the United States in 1945—most of them Jewish—attempts to expand that limited program met with public resistance until it became apparent that most of the subsequent arrivals would be Christians. In the end, four hundred fifteen thousand European refugees were admitted under the Displaced Persons Act of 1948, and another two hundred fourteen thousand under the Refugee Relief Act of 1953. These were not simply acts of humanitarian generosity; U.S. leaders did not want to see refugees sent back to countries which had become part of the Soviet bloc, with which the United States was now locked in Cold War struggle.[9]

U.S. refugee admissions remained politically polarized well after the onset of the Cold War. Victims of communist regimes with which the

United States had hostile relations tended to be admitted. For instance, the United States admitted thirty-eight thousand refugees from Hungary after Soviet troops crushed an anti-communist uprising in 1956. And when the communist revolution led by Fidel Castro in Cuba against the U.S.-backed dictator Fulgencio Batista came out on top in 1959, the resulting waves of refugees over the years that followed were admitted to the United States and settled mostly in Miami. From 1962 to 1979, roughly seven hundred thousand arrived. In the case of communist regimes in Indochina, hundreds of thousands of refugees came to the United States after 1975—four hundred thousand by 1979, with many more coming during the 1980s.[10]

Ironically, many of these Indochinese refugees had already been uprooted in the course of the U.S. war in Vietnam, during which, by 1969, the U.S. military had dropped so many bombs that South Vietnam had become one of the three most heavily bombed countries in history—the other two being Vietnam's neighbors, Laos and Cambodia, which the United States was also bombing. In South Vietnam, a country where people had deep economic, social, and religious ties to their land, U.S. authorities forcibly relocated the civilian population in order to physically separate them from the insurgents whom U.S. soldiers were battling.[11] Thanks in large part to the bombing and the U.S. program of forcible relocation, by 1975 more than half of South Vietnam's population had been internally displaced at least once during the previous twenty years. So it's important to keep in mind that even after the communist victories in Vietnam, Cambodia, and Laos, the refugees admitted to the United States from all three countries were fleeing communist states built upon the social and economic wreckage left behind by the United States.[12]

The U.S. government adopted a very different approach to the victims of right-wing regimes which it supported. These refugees were not even acknowledged as such—lest the government be forced to admit that it was helping military dictatorships kill and torture their own people and drive them out of their own country. This is exactly what took place in El Salvador and Guatemala during the 1980s. In contrast, after the leftist Sandinista revolution in Nicaragua toppled the U.S.-backed dictator Anastasio Somoza in 1979, relatively few refugees sought to leave the country. But the Reagan Administration prolonged the conflict, trying to topple the Sandinista government through an economic blockade and by backing right-wing guerrillas known as "contras."[13]

It was not until 1980 that the United States created a single refugee program—as opposed to separate programs for each group being admitted—and finally adopted a definition of the term "refugee" which was close to the one codified by the United Nations in 1951.[14] As the Refugee Act of 1980 defined it, a refugee was "any person unable or unwilling to return to his or her country because of persecution or a well-founded fear of persecution on account of race, religion, nationality, membership in a particular social group, or political opinion."[15]

As the definition of the term suggests, all refugees share certain experiences in common. But refugees also come from an extraordinarily diverse range of societies, and they live through unique historical moments. In the 1880s, for instance, hundreds of thousands of Russian Jews fled their homes in the face of political violence. The assassination of Tsar Alexander II in 1881 was blamed by the Russian government on Jews and used as a pretext for murderous anti-Jewish pogroms, or riots. Most of the refugees seeking to escape these attacks made their way to the United States, enduring grueling and dangerous journeys that culminated at Ellis Island in New York. More than a hundred years later, at the dawn of the twenty-first century, hundreds of thousands of refugees from Iraq fled the horrific destruction wrought by the U.S.-led invasion and chaotic aftermath of sectarian warfare and terror attacks. It was to the United States that tens of thousands of these refugees fled.

The Pogroms

In February of 1880, when Tsar Alexander II narrowly escaped bombs planted in his Winter Palace by socialist revolutionaries, government officials resorted to a time-honored technique for distracting the public: they blamed the Jews. More precisely, the head of the Russian security police, P. A. Cherevin, embarked upon the fanciful pursuit of an imagined international conspiracy of Jews to assassinate the emperor. As historian John Doyle Klier describes it, Cherevin instructed authorities in those Russian provinces where Jews were allowed to live to hunt for a "universal Jewish kahal"—a secretive body which was allegedly supported by all Jews and which pursued aims "inimical to the Christian population." For good measure, the Poles were also accused of having revolutionary intentions, but Jews were the principal scapegoats. According to Cherevin's soon-to-be chief, N.P. Ignatiev, a Polish Jewish cabal in St. Petersburg controlled banks, the stock exchange, the legal profession, and countless members of the press.[16]

The unease that many Russians felt towards the Jewish population stemmed in part from the belief that all Jews were religious fanatics intent upon the economic exploitation of Russians. The charge of fanaticism was rationalized in terms of the differences in dress and language, as well as differences in family and community organization, that were apparent among Jews in eastern Europe. Many Russians assumed that Jews felt superior to non-Jews and thus lacked any loyalty to the nation or state. Moreover, Jewish men were portrayed as being taught from a young age to cheat and exploit non-Jews. Russians also commonly believed that Jews led a parasitic way of life as peddlers, money lenders, and tavern keepers. As a result, many Russians thought that Jews were in urgent need of reform in order to transform them into good Russian subjects.

What to do with the Jews in Russia—the so-called "Jewish Question"—dated back to 1772, when the partition of Poland placed Jewish communities within the Russian Empire for the first time. And Russians were still struggling to find an answer to that question when Alexander II came to power in 1855 and began implementing his Great Reforms to modernize economic, social, and political life throughout Russia. As part of these reforms, rights were expanded for those Jews deemed productive, such as urban artisans, large-scale merchants, and those with special skills or advanced education. Conversely, new restrictions were introduced on allegedly unproductive Jews such as tavern keepers.

During this era of sweeping reforms, there were two Russian points of view regarding Jews. "Judeophobes" were obsessed by the notion that there was an enormous anti-Christian conspiracy among the Jews, orchestrated by the "international kahal." Some even believed that Jews ritually murdered Christian children. However, there were also

"Judeophiles"—particularly in the early days of the Reform Era—who defended the use of the reform process to solve the Jewish Question. By the end of Alexander II's reign, there were clear indications that the legal status of Jews was about to change, but no one knew for sure what kind of change it would be. Differences of opinion on this topic did not fall along clear-cut ideological lines. For example, there were Judeophobes who favored abolishing the restrictions on where Jews could and couldn't live with the argument that all parts of the empire should have to bear the burden of hosting a Jewish population. Meanwhile, many otherwise liberal commentators thought the existing restrictions should be kept in place so as to save the hapless and helpless Russian peasantry from exploitation by the more market-savvy Jews.

Adding to these muddled perspectives, the neat dividing line that had traditionally been drawn between the Jewish masses (assumed by Judeophiles and Judeophobes alike to be ignorant religious zealots living largely separate and apart from mainstream Russian society) and the Jewish intelligentsia (an educated and presumably enlightened elite) was breaking down. However, as the Judeophobes became more extreme in their conspiracy theories, the Jewish intelligentsia found itself defending the Jewish masses. Judeophobes, predictably enough, countered with the accusation that the Jewish intelligentsia was also in on the vast conspiracy. And as more and more Jews entered public schooling within the empire, Judeophobes accused them of filling the classrooms and forcing out Christians. Yet how all of this rhetorical warfare would affect public policy remained murky. Contradictory signals were emanating from different government ministries.

It was at this point, when change of some kind was just about to materialize, that Alexander II was assassinated in a bomb attack on March 1, 1881. The conspirators were promptly hanged in public on April 3, at which point public speculation swirled as to how the revolutionaries would respond to the execution of their comrades. The situation was further complicated by timing. The Russian Orthodox Easter, with all of its attendant public festivities, was coming up rapidly on April 12. Immediately following Easter was Bright Week; a holiday marked by celebrations that at times became riotous. And, to top it all off, this time of year was Paschal season for Jews, during which Christian–Jewish conflict that occasionally turned into rioting was fairly common even under ordinary circumstances. Matters were not made any easier by the fact that the new tsar, Alexander III, had yet to give any indication of how he planned to rule. This ambiguity was mirrored in the fact that reformist and reactionary factions within the government were jockeying for position as Alexander III assumed power. In short, Russian society was a powder keg just waiting for a lit match.

Documenting what happened next during the spasms of violence that quickly ensued is no simple matter. This is not surprising considering the conflicting impressions that different people have of what is going on in the midst of violent chaos. In particular, there is a divide between what government officials report to their superiors and what journalists report to their editors. News stories often report rumor as fact and are politically colored by the ideological affiliation of the paper. Officials submitting reports are motivated by the desire to make themselves look good. In the case of the pogroms against the Jews, this divergence of press and state is particularly apparent in accounts of rape. According to the newspapers of the time, rape was widespread during the pogroms. Yet it rarely appears in government reports. Newspapers might have had an interest in exaggerating the incidence of rape in order to sensationalize their stories. Misogynist government officials might have downplayed the extent to which rape occurred because they didn't view it as particularly important. But rape was a serious crime in Russia, so it is unlikely that all of the officials reporting to the tsar would ignore it—especially if, as so many newspapers said, it was widespread and accompanied by other gruesome forms of torture. Still, problems of credibility notwithstanding, government reports, cross-checked with each another and with press accounts, are the most reliable sources of information available on the turmoil which followed soon after the assassination of Alexander II.

The first wave of anti-Jewish pogroms began in Elisavetgrad, a town of forty-five thousand containing a total of eighty-seven police officers. Officials heard rumors that an attack on Jews was imminent and the police were reinforced with a detachment of military troops on April 10. Moreover, shops, taverns, and inns were ordered to close for the first three days of Bright Week. Officials had to reassure the populace that this was occurring not because the Jews had bought the holiday, as rumor had it, but as a gesture of respect to the recently assassinated tsar. When nothing riotous occurred, the troops withdrew, and chaos soon followed. A fight broke out between a Jewish tavern owner and a Christian customer. The commotion drew a crowd, which ignored the orders of a police sergeant to disperse. Instead, they shouted "The Yids are beating our people!" and proceeded to attack Jewish targets. The mob headed to the marketplace, smashed Jewish shop windows, and threw the merchandise out into the street. Some Jewish shopkeepers tried to defend their stores using crowbars and axes, but to no avail. The rioters next moved on to attacking Jewish homes—removing furniture and smashing it in the street. Officials, realizing that the police could not possibly restore order on their own, desperately requested that two squadrons of troops return to town. Meanwhile, police and troops already there rushed the crowd and managed to arrest twenty rioters, but it did little good at this point.

The rioters headed to back streets and outlying neighborhoods, where they continued their attacks on Jews. Military reinforcements finally arrived and managed to restore some semblance of order, including the defusing of a potentially catastrophic situation at the main synagogue. Inside was a crowd of terrified Jews seeking safety; outside was a mob throwing stones at the windows. There were only occasional outbursts of violence that night, but the rioting resumed the next morning on a massive scale. The authorities responded in a somewhat haphazard fashion at first before troops tried to systematically secure the town that night. They met with limited success. For instance, they chased off one large mob (about a thousand people) by firing over their heads. But in other cases, when they tried to arrest people, they found themselves showered with rocks and paving stones by angry rioters. And the troops were wary of being too aggressive given the presence of many onlookers, including women and children. As a result, the rioters were left with the impression that their actions were permissible. In the end, one Jew was beaten to death by rioters, while others were badly beaten or thrown from the upper floors of their homes. According to official accounts, 418 Jewish homes were attacked and 290 shops and market stalls were trashed.

Authorities arrested 601 people. In addition to the one beating death, two rioters died of alcohol poisoning.

Pogroms tended to spread from one locale to another via rail lines, highways, and rivers. So it was not surprising that, on April 16 and 17, anti-Jewish rioting broke out in two villages within walking distance of Elisavetgrad. From there they spread to farther removed villages in rural areas. Most of this first wave of pogroms had dissipated by the end of April. In September, an official report on the pogroms recorded 832 Jewish homes attacked, 434 commercial buildings damaged, 992 people arrested, and no fatalities beyond the three in Elisavetgrad. Officials were worried that the pogroms would spread to Odessa, which was a pogrom-prone city to begin with. And so provinces with significant Jewish populations were ordered to prepare, and troops were dispatched to reinforce local police in towns where pogrom rumors were running rampant. But it wasn't enough.

The second wave of pogroms began in Kiev, which not only had a large Jewish population, but an active socialist revolutionary movement that might view rioting as an opportunity to foment a broader uprising against the state. The violence began with fights between Jewish and Christian children, leading the police to close taverns and disperse any gatherings of people on the street as a preventive measure. Jews were advised to stay indoors. And yet street fights began to spread. On April 26 a fight between a Christian and a Jew served as the spark for the next wave of pogroms. A crowd looted Jewish businesses in a marketplace, shouting—among other things—"Beat the Jews who killed our tsar," and then scattered throughout the city, attacking Jewish homes and beating the occupants. Many Jews fled to the homes of Christian neighbors, who had placed crosses or other religious icons in their windows to identify themselves as non-Jews. Troops protected a couple of well-off neighborhoods, but not the rest of the city.

Although the rioting subsided that night and in the predawn hours, it resumed at daybreak. This time troops dispersed the crowds with whips and pikes. That day, an announcement from the governor general was circulated which stated that the army and police were authorized to use deadly force in the face of more rioting. That afternoon, when a mob attacked a Jewish-owned brewery while throwing stones at nearby troops, the troops responded by firing into the crowd, killing a woman and wounding three men. As this news circulated throughout the city, the pogrom died down. By the end of the pogrom's second day, more than one thousand people had been arrested. For the authorities, the pogrom was made even more menacing when police raided an underground printing press and found a couple of socialist revolutionaries urging the people to attack the Russian authorities rather than the Jews.

The Kiev pogrom ended on April 28, but the authorities realized they had to direct their attention to railway workers to stop the violence from spreading, given that railroad stations were the focus of the worst violence at the onset of the Kiev pogrom. Indeed, by the second day after the end of the pogrom, rioting was breaking out at a number of rail depots quite a distance from the city, with railway workers themselves often central players in the pogroms. In these locales beyond Kiev, the level of violence escalated. In Smela, for example, mobs killed four Jews and, on May 3, troops firing into a crowd of rioters killed two people.

Despite the higher death toll in the second wave of pogroms, the situation seemed to be under control by mid-May. Tavern hours were restricted prior to religious holidays and regional fairs. People were lectured on the unacceptability of attacking Jews. Pogrom trials were rushed to make examples of the convicted rioters, while troops were kept on standby. And authorities in Kiev expelled unauthorized Jewish residents. But it was clear that intense anti-Jewish animosity remained.

On June 7 in Pereiaslav—where the third wave of pogroms would begin—hundreds of residents signed a petition calling for the expulsion of Jews who had settled in the town without permission—most of whom had fled the Kiev pogrom. Authorities rejected the request as illegal, but declined to let the public know about this decision. In the meantime, street fights broke out between Christians and Jews. On June 30, one such fight erupted into a full-blown riot in the marketplace, complete with a huge brawl and attacks on Jewish shops. When a Jewish merchant fired on the mob, the rioters were whipped into a frenzy and began destroying Jewish property. Troops stamped out the riot and arrested twenty-six people—many of whom were released the next day. Although the pogrom did not end for good until July 2, there were no fatalities, but 166 homes were damaged.

Throughout July, however, pogroms spread to rural areas surrounding Pereiaslav, starting with attacks on Jewish taverns and progressing to looting and destruction of Jewish property. It went much worse in Borispol, where the troops patrolling the marketplace were attacked with stones by a drunken mob. The troops fired and used their sabers in self-defense, killing five people. Likewise, a pogrom in Nezhin ultimately left eleven rioters dead, shot by troops trying to put down the pogrom while defending themselves from enraged rioters throwing rocks and bottles.

While this marked the last actual wave of pogroms, there were two more large-scale pogroms in major urban areas that did not spread elsewhere. The first, which started on December 25, 1881, occurred in Warsaw (in what was then the kingdom of Poland). It began when someone yelled "Fire!" during morning services at one of the city's largest churches. A stampede of frightened worshipers ensued in which twenty-eight people died. By the late afternoon, a rumor was making the rounds that a Jewish pickpocket was to blame for the fatal stampede. Allegedly, he had yelled "Fire!" when he was apprehended in the church so that he could escape in the resulting confusion. Fueled by this rumor, gangs of youths began attacking Jewish taverns and homes in the evening, and continued to do so until December 27, when troops finally put down the rioting. Fighting landed twenty-four Christians and twenty-two Jews in hospitals, with one of the injured Jews later dying.

The second major pogrom took place in Balta and erupted on March 29, 1882. Roughly half of the town's twenty thousand residents were Jews, yet the entire police force of the town numbered thirty-six, and only sixty-three soldiers were available for riot duty. Exactly how the pogrom started is unknown, although fights and stone throwing between Christians and Jews in front of the main church were its first manifestations. At this point, Jews far outnumbered Christians in the altercation. Authorities managed to disperse the crowd and arrested both Christians and Jews, but the Christian detainees were soon released. A rumor then spread around town that Jews had vandalized the Orthodox Church. The authorities blundered by accepting and repeating this rumor in official pronouncements, and then compounded the error by keeping troops clustered next to the church in order to protect it, while leaving the rest of the town at the mercy of the rioters. The next day, authorities made their biggest mistake: they recruited five hundred peasants to help restore order, gave them clubs, and sent them on their way with no precise orders. The peasants promptly joined the pogrom and vastly expanded its scope. Most Jewish property was looted or destroyed by midday. The death toll was anywhere from four to twelve, of whom one or two were Jewish. A defining feature of this pogrom, however, was rape. Three women pressed charges against their rapists, but the total number of victims may have been twenty-eight (including, allegedly, a mother and daughter). Although the Balta pogrom didn't trigger a wave of rioting, there were scattered incidents in the countryside of vandalism, rape, and fights—some resulting in fatalities.

With all of this transpiring, many Jews fled Russia in search of a safer home. In the summer of 1881, they began moving from small towns to big cities, and from the province of Volynia across the Austrian border into the Galician town of Brody (which had an established Jewish community ready to help the initial flow of refugees). International and national groups helped as well. On May 26, after the Kiev pogrom, the Paris-based Alliance Israélite Universelle issued a worldwide call for help. On August 14, the Alliance contracted with the Antwerp agency Henri Strauss to send five hundred refugees from Brody to the United States. Most of the refugees sent across the Atlantic were tradesmen and poorly skilled craftsmen—much to the dismay of U.S. authorities who complained that the new arrivals were unaccustomed to heavy labor. But false rumors swirled of what the Alliance allegedly had to offer (such as a free trip to the United States), so refugees kept flocking into Brody. The frequent attempts of the Alliance to dispel such rumors had little impact.

As a result, tensions between the American Jewish groups and European Jewish groups were high. The Europeans explained that the emigration crisis was beyond their control, and that the United States should expect substantial flows for years to come. The U.S. side was displeased by the quality of the refugees being selected (too many widows with children, for instance, rather than able-bodied working men)—and by the fact that Austrians and Galicians were making their way into the mix. The Americans emphasized that coming to the United States was not a panacea for the problems of Russian Jews, and that comparatively few could benefit. And they were angered by the rampant rumors of the riches to be had in the United States. The Americans demanded that fewer refugees be sent each month, lest legions more be inspired to seek refuge in America. This forced a temporary pause, and then a slowdown, in the migration of refugees from Russia. But it would by no means mark the end of Jewish migration from Europe to the United States.

THE INTERPRETERS

The U.S.-led invasion of Iraq in 2003 quickly threw the country into chaos. The armed forces of the United States and its coalition partners succeeded in toppling the Iraqi government, but had no workable plan to create a new governing structure that might take its place and guarantee the security of the Iraqi people.[17] As Human Right Watch points out, "coalition troops were quickly overwhelmed by the enormity of the task of maintaining public order in Iraq. Looting was pervasive. Arms caches were raided and emptied. Violence was rampant."[18] To top it all off, the overwhelming majority of the troops deployed in Iraq were soldiers trained to kill enemy combatants—not to police an occupied nation. And so a steady stream of lethal mishaps occurred in which coalition troops (as well as private contractors) fired on civilians.[19]

Not surprisingly, large numbers of Iraqi civilians died in the course of the bombing campaign that was the centerpiece of the invasion.[20] According to Iraq Body Count, the civilian death toll came to roughly ten thousand.[21] But far more than that have died in the years of sectarian violence and terror attacks that followed as different armed groups vied for control of the country. By March 2015, the civilian body count from armed conflict of all kinds since the invasion stood at more than one hundred seventy-four thousand.[22]

As violence engulfed their nation, millions of Iraqis fled their homes. Most went to other parts of the country, but hundreds of thousands sought refuge in Jordan, Turkey, and Lebanon. This already horrendous situation was made even worse with the rise of the Islamic State (ISIS) in Iraq and neighboring Syria, which not only caused more Iraqis to flee from a new source of violence, but propelled many Syrian refugees into Iraq since even that war-torn country was a safer bet than Syria. The flood of Syrian refugees, especially those who made it to Europe, soon dominated world attention and eclipsed the plight of the Iraqis. But the situation of Iraqis remained dire. In 2015, there were two hundred forty thousand Iraqi refugees in neighboring countries, while another 3.2 million were internally displaced.[23]

Tens of thousands of refugees from Iraq were eventually resettled in the United States. Among these, one group in particular stands out for the unique role they played in the U.S. occupation of Iraq: the interpreters. These were generally young, single, college-educated men and women from urban, middle-class backgrounds. They not only served as language interpreters for U.S. troops, but cultural interpreters as well. This was a critical—and dangerous—function considering that U.S. troops had little to no understanding of the people they sometimes imagined they were setting free. As anthropologist Madeline Otis Campbell describes them, the interpreters were constantly immersed in suspicion and mistrust. U.S. troops were forever unsure of their true loyalties, while many Iraqis viewed them as traitors for helping the foreign troops who were occupying the country. The interpreters even mistrusted each other; unsure of who was really pro-American and who harbored sympathies for the insurgents fighting the U.S. occupation.[24]

The interpreters who Campbell came to know, first in her role as a refugee officer in Iraq and then as an ethnographer in New England, were born in the 1970s and 1980s. As such, they were, quite literally, children of war. They had grown up with the bloody Iran–Iraq War of 1980–1988 (which began with Iraq's invasion of Iran and killed between two hundred fifty thousand and five hundred thousand Iraqis), the Gulf War with the United States in late 1990 and early 1991 (beginning with Iraq's invasion of Kuwait), more than a decade of crippling economic sanctions spearheaded by the United States, and then the U.S. invasion in 2003 and subsequent military occupation which presided over an anarchic spiral of violence.

War Refugees at Zakany Railway Station. Refugees Are Arriving Constantly to Hungary On the Way to Germany. 5 October 2015 in Zakany, Hungary
IMAGE © ISTOCK.COM/CSAKISTI

While these relatively young people may have ended up working for the Americans, the vast majority were not fans of the U.S. invasion or U.S. armed forces. Rather, in the economic wreckage left by the U.S. invasion, they found that their most marketable skills were knowledge of the English language combined with firsthand understanding of Iraqi society—and the U.S. military was hiring. Some were also motivated by the desire to restore a semblance of law and order to their devastated country.

In the eyes of U.S. military authorities, these interpreters were much more than language translators. They were cultural brokers; helping U.S. troops to harness the power of those cultural traits seen as wartime assets, while subduing traits seen as cultural threats. The military went so far as to put soldiers through simulation camps in the deserts of California and Arizona in which Iraqi refugees often played the role of generic Iraqi civilians so that the soldiers could learn a few Arabic phrases and, just as importantly, acquire the cultural skills needed to gain the trust of ordinary Iraqis. U.S. authorities even implemented a program in 2007 called the Human Terrain System that enlisted U.S. social scientists in the planning of military operations. Unfortunately, what the U.S. military ended up doing more often than not was stereotyping Iraqis as violent cultural traditionalists and religious fundamentalists.

The importance of understanding Iraqi culture in the eyes of those U.S. officials who were managing the U.S. occupation actually granted the interpreters a measure of power. By appealing to the power of culture, for instance, interpreters could persuade U.S. troops to provide better treatment to someone they had detained. Campbell recalls a story told by an interpreter who thought it wrong for a U.S. Marine to lock two detainees to a pole outside and leave them there overnight. So he lied and told the Marines that wetting your pants is a highly shameful act in Iraqi culture and that the detainees therefore should be kept indoors and allowed to use a toilet. On another occasion, a U.S. officer told an interpreter to tell a sheik that he had to surrender all of his weapons. The interpreter knew that would sound extremely disrespectful, so—instead—he told the sheik that the officer wanted his advice on how to deal with illegal weapons in the village. This intentional mistranslation avoided what could have become a very volatile situation and got the officer and the sheik to start speaking with one another in a non-confrontational manner.

Despite such efforts to help Iraqis, the interpreters were not exactly loved by much of the local population. For this reason, they took care to conceal their faces when they were working. At the time Campbell met them, the preferred means of doing so were to wear military uniforms, helmets, and goggles. Wearing some sort of mask not only kept them safe from militants who would kill them for working with the U.S. occupation. It also allowed them to play whatever character was most appropriate in whatever situation they found themselves; such as adopting one persona in Sunni areas and another in Shi'a areas.

The dependence of U.S. military authorities on the skills of the interpreters was evident from the earliest days of the occupation, when Titan Communications Corp. hired more than eight thousand of them—and paid them each $12,000 per year for performing one of the most dangerous civilian jobs in the country. One investigation found that from the beginning of the war up until the troop surge of 2007, roughly 360 interpreters were killed and more than 1,200 seriously injured. The deteriorating security situation in the country by 2006 and 2007 led many interpreters to leave not only their jobs, but the country. However, not all interpreting jobs entailed equal risk. Jobs on military bases were relatively safe, while going on U.S. combat missions was extremely dangerous. Female interpreters were, in almost all cases, assigned to non-combat duties on bases, while men worked both on base and on patrol. While those who worked on base were generally safer from militant attacks, the women interpreters faced threats of another kind. They were often harassed, pressured for sex, and sometimes raped. Having lived through the horrors of the U.S. invasion and its chaotic aftermath, these interpreters then had to avoid sexual assault by soldiers with whom, or for whom, they worked.

Nevertheless, many of the male interpreters often came to view the U.S. soldiers with whom they worked as brothers in arms. This bond was based in large part on the belief that they were, together, helping to rebuild Iraq. The interpreters had to look beyond a war they opposed, and behavior on the part of U.S. troops that they found unacceptable, for the sake of giving their people a voice in the face of military occupation. Campbell recounts that one interpreter quit his job three different times, but kept going back because of his conviction that the Iraqi people needed someone to look out for them in their dealings with heavily armed and sometimes trigger-happy U.S. troops who knew nothing about Iraq.

In the end, the interpreters whom Campbell interviewed applied for refugee status in the United States because of explicit death threats from insurgents, rumors that their names were on a hit list, or a nagging fear that it was only a matter of time before they'd be receiving death threats. Fortunately for them, there was an expedited program for Iraqis who had worked with the U.S. military. Those interpreters who could establish a threat of persecution if they remained in Iraq, as well as no links to terrorist activity or the persecution of others, had a reasonably good chance of making it to the United States.

CHAPTER TWO

Hand to Mouth

WHILE MANY PEOPLE IN THE WORLD ARE FLEEING VIOLENCE, OTHERS are fleeing from poverty. This can be a dire situation in which family members are going hungry and one or more of them must journey elsewhere to find jobs if they are all to survive. Or, more often, it is a situation of chronic deprivation in which the members of a family are managing to keep their heads above water. But they have little hope of climbing any further up the socioeconomic ladder unless they journey somewhere else, or send someone abroad who can provide them with a financial infusion by sending money back home.

In general, these economic migrants are not the poorest of the poor in their home countries. The poorest people in any society don't usually have enough resources at their disposal to migrate to another country. But even those fortunate enough to have the money needed to escape are leaving behind a dismal situation in which impoverishment is never far away. Moreover, economic migrants don't generally possess much formal education or job skills which would be classified as "advanced" by the standards of modern industrial societies. So their job prospects within the modern industrial societies to which they migrate are fairly limited, at least in the beginning.

THE DAWN OF A NEW ERA
At the broadest level, migration from Europe to the United States in the nineteenth century had much to do with the Industrial Revolution. As described by historian Roger Daniels and sociologists Alejandro Portes and

Ruben G. Rumbaut, industrialization progressively made its way through Great Britain, Germany, Scandinavia, Italy, and eastern Europe, leaving in its wake peasants who were displaced from their lands by mechanized agriculture.[1] Unable to even grow their own food anymore, these former peasants had no choice but to work for wages in the factories that were sprouting up in the cities, either in their home countries or abroad. Meanwhile, in the United States, capitalists who were building factories for the mass production of goods needed a bountiful supply of low-cost labor to run those factories. They found this supply of workers among the displaced peasants of Europe who were willing to sail across the Atlantic Ocean for jobs.

By the end of the century, Italians and eastern Europeans were flocking to the United States by the hundreds of thousands to become the human raw materials of the American Industrial Revolution. Of course, the arrival of so many migrants was made possible by the invention of the steamship and the rise of migrant transport into a big business. From 1880 to 1920, roughly 4.1 million Italian immigrants arrived in this country, as did large but indeterminate numbers of Germans, Austrians, Hungarians, Romanians, Russians, and Poles. While the majority of these migrants were either trying to rise out of poverty or at least significantly improve what they perceived to be a low standard of living, Jews from eastern Europe had an added motivation: escape from religious persecution. Regardless of the motivations that immigrants had for coming, many native-born U.S. workers—who perceived their livelihoods as threatened by unwanted job competition from immigrant newcomers—responded with xenophobic and racist hatred.

But Europe was not the only source of workers for the U.S. industrial machine. In 1848, following Mexico's defeat in the Mexican-American War, the United States took nearly half of Mexico's territory, encompassing New Mexico, Arizona, California, Nevada, and Utah, plus portions of Colorado and Wyoming. This also marked the start of the California Gold Rush, which led to high demand for miners that was met by contractors who went to southern China and recruited workers. And when U.S. railroad companies undertook the ambitious task of linking the Pacific Coast of the United States with the Atlantic Coast, the enormous demand for railroad workers was also filled by Chinese contract workers.

When the railroads linking the two halves of the country were complete, Chinese railroad workers were out of a job. They tried their hand at working the fields of California farms, but the racist backlash against their presence forced them out. This nativist sentiment culminated in the 1882 Chinese Exclusion Act, which completely barred further migration from China to the United States. Chinese men moved to the cities and formed tight-knit communities that would one day be known as "Chinatowns," where they made ends meet by operating laundries and restaurants.

With Chinese workers now out of bounds, California's farmers began to import workers from Japan instead. The Japanese workers were not only efficient, but quite entrepreneurial. They started to acquire their own land and farm for themselves. The nativist outcry over this unexpected and unwelcome development resulted in the passage of two state laws in the California legislature—in 1913 and 1920—which made it illegal for the Japanese to own land. Japanese workers and farmers followed the lead of the Chinese and moved to the cities, where they scattered throughout the urban landscape and operated hotels, grocery stores, dry cleaners, and a variety of other enterprises.

The Foreign Element in New York—the Chinese Colony, Mott Street
DRAWN BY W. BENGOUGH. LC-USZ62-107167

Native-born farmers, now denied access to Japanese workers, started recruiting Mexicans to work in the fields. From the farmers' perspective, using Mexican workers had one important advantage over relying on Chinese or Japanese workers: they lived just across the border in Mexico, so they could just go home when the harvest was over and they weren't needed anymore. The importance of these workers in keeping U.S. farms running must have been apparent even to the Congressmen who passed the anti-immigrant National Origins Act in 1924, because immigration from Mexico and other Latin American countries was exempt from the limits imposed on immigration from all of the other countries outside of northern and western Europe.

The Great Depression, World War II, and racist immigration laws brought most immigration to a halt between 1930 and 1940. But farmers still needed someone to work the fields. During this period, the government implemented the Bracero program—a massive temporary worker program which brought millions of Mexicans to the United States to work the fields under inhumane conditions and then shipped them back over the border when the work was done. Mexicans who crossed the border illegally (or who failed to leave) were deported in an effort to reduce the unemployment rate among native-born workers. In the early 1950's, for instance, the Immigration and Naturalization Service (INS) staged "Operation Wetback," which expelled 3.8 million Mexicans from the country.

The blatant racism of the 1924 National Origins Act was rejected in 1965 with passage of the Hart-Celler Act—a law infused with the spirit of the civil rights movement which scrapped quotas based on national origin. The law set a ceiling of one hundred seventy thousand on immigration from the Eastern Hemisphere (with a limit of twenty thousand per country) and one hundred twenty thousand from the Western Hemisphere (with no per-country limit). However, in 1976, the per-country quota of twenty thousand was applied to the Western Hemisphere as well. This made little sense. Setting the same limits on immigration from Mexico as from Mongolia ignored the depth of the economic, social, and historical ties between Mexico and the United States. So when the U.S. market for low-end jobs in construction, restaurants, landscaping, and child care began to grow by leaps and bounds over the decades that followed, drawing millions of workers from Mexico and other Latin American countries as well as many from Asian nations, the legal channels for immigration were grossly inadequate to handle the actual level of demand. The result was the steady rise in the number of undocumented immigrants, attracted by plentiful jobs that, despite low pay, provided them with better economic prospects than they faced back home.[2]

The U.S. government attempted to address the problem of undocumented immigration in 1986 through the Immigration Reform and Control Act (IRCA). While IRCA granted legal status to roughly three million undocumented immigrants already living in the United States, it failed to create new legal channels for immigrants to enter the country sufficient to satisfy the growing demand for workers to fill less-skilled jobs. And so the problem of undocumented immigration resurfaced almost immediately. The number of undocumented immigrants rose to more than twelve million in 2007 before falling to around eleven million in 2009.[3]

The failure of IRCA to deal with this issue head-on was particularly ironic since the U.S., Mexican, and Canadian governments were at the same time encouraging the economic integration of all three countries, culminating in the North American Free Trade Agreement (NAFTA) in 1994. Economic integration fosters more migration—not less, yet U.S. politicians lacked the will to overhaul the immigration system in the same manner they had overhauled the trade regime. However, they did find the will to sink billions of dollars into immigration enforcement—especially border enforcement. With every passing year, there were more "boots on the ground," miles of border fencing, helicopters, airplanes, and all manner of high-tech gadgets devoted to detecting unauthorized border crossings.[4] From 1986 to 2012, the federal government spent $187 billion on immigration enforcement.[5]

The upshot was that job-seeking men and women from Mexico and elsewhere in Latin America—as well as the Caribbean, Asia, and Africa—kept heading for the United States because that's where so many jobs were located. In the absence of visas to come legally, and despite the ever-expanding apparatus of immigration enforcement, they made

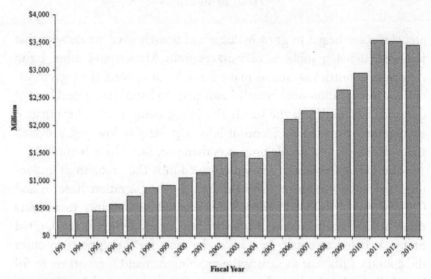

U.S. Border Patrol Budget, FY 1993–2013

SOURCE: U.S. BORDER PATROL, "U.S. BORDER PATROL FISCAL YEAR BUDGET STATISTICS," JANUARY 27, 2014.

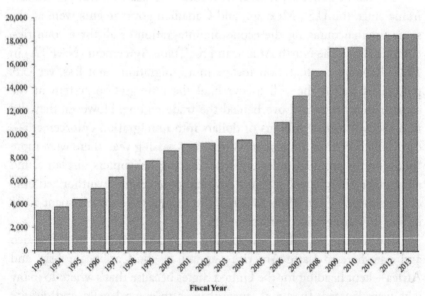

Number of U.S. Border Patrol Agents Stationed along Southwest Border, FY 1993–2013

SOURCE: U.S. BORDER PATROL, "U.S. BORDER PATROL FISCAL YEAR STAFFING STATISTICS," JANUARY 27, 2014.

the decision to come without a visa, or to overstay a tourist or student visa when it expired. As of 2014, there were about eight million undocumented immigrants in the U.S. labor force, accounting for 5 percent of all workers in the country.[6] Some policymakers and political commentators have proposed addressing this issue rationally: by overhauling the immigration system and its arbitrary, inflexible numerical caps. They argue that the "enforcement-only" approach to undocumented immigration is inappropriate in dealing with people who are coming to work in order to provide for their families.

Others want to fix the problem in a more unyielding fashion: building a giant wall along the southern U.S. border and ramping up deportations. The rhetoric of immigration enforcement tends to be militaristic, with the "war against terrorism" and the "last line of defense" continually invoked in justifying a punishing response to everyone who tries to cross the border without a visa, regardless of their motivations. Such rhetoric is understandable in the post-9/11 era. But it is misplaced in most cases. The overwhelming majority of the modern economic migrants who have crossed or attempted to cross the U.S.-Mexico border into the United States are no more of a threat than were the Irish migrants fleeing the Irish Potato Famine in the mid-eighteen hundreds.

THE GREAT FAMINE

The potato blight first struck Ireland in 1845, but only claimed part of the crop since much of it had already been harvested. That was not the case in 1846, when the crop failure was total—claiming as much as 90 percent of the potatoes grown on the island. At this point, according to historians Jay P. Dolan and James S. Donnelly, Jr., starvation began to spread, with the omnipresent smell of rotting potatoes an apt metaphor for what was happening to the dirt poor Irish families that grew most of them.[7] The potato crop was marginal the following year, in 1847, or Black '47, as it was known, due to the extent of the starvation and disease which followed the failure of the crop. Adding insult to injury, the winter of 1846–1847 was particularly cold, and half the potato crop was again lost to blight in 1848. At that point, cholera began to spread throughout the countryside. Yet things got even worse when the potato crops failed for each of the next two years. Over the course of the five years that the Great Famine endured, from 1846 to 1851, 1.1 million Irish men, women, and children died of starvation and disease. Another 1.5 million emigrated, with most bound for the United States.

It would be a mistake to attribute all of the death and suffering which occurred during the Great Famine to the spread of a potato fungus. This disaster was long in the making, and was very much man-made. The potato, which was brought to Ireland from Peru in the sixteenth century, was the staple of the Irish diet by the mid-eighteenth century. By the time the famine struck, the potato was the main source of food for more than half of Ireland's population. Out of the 8.5 million people living in Ireland as of 1845, 4.7 million relied predominantly on potatoes—and, of these, 3.3 million depended almost exclusively on potatoes, supplemented at times by some milk or fish. Landless agricultural laborers, small landholders, and tenants living on less than twenty acres of land were the most heavily dependent on potatoes. In fact, those without land accounted for more than one-quarter of the population. Many were "bound" laborers obligated to work a certain number of days for a given farmer in exchange for a tiny house and small plot of ground.

The rise in poverty and potato dependency coincided with rapid population growth starting in the mid-eighteenth century. In fact, between 1750 and 1845, the Irish population ballooned from 2.6 million to 8.5 million, a trend which drove rents higher and wages lower, while leading to the fragmentation of land holdings into very small plots. Moreover, industry withered in the Irish countryside in the face of competition from more rapidly industrializing parts of the United Kingdom, which contributed to serious underemployment. The central problem was not the state of the Irish economy as a whole, but the massive inequality which characterized it. When the famine hit, at least half of the population was already poverty stricken.

Potatoes grew readily under even poor conditions, and with a minimum of human labor required. They were therefore the perfect subsistence crop—or so it seemed—to the masses of rural poor who lived on small plots of land. When this crop failed, there was no backup, and very few people had the money to buy food to replace their rotting crops. The result was catastrophic. There were accounts of entire families, gaunt and skeletal, huddled together in their tiny homes, waiting to die. A local priest in a hard-hit county wrote, "They were dying by the dozens in the street."[8]

The British, who ruled Ireland at the time, responded tepidly to this crisis, to say the least. On the one hand, the abundant oat crop that was harvested in 1845 was exported rather than used to feed Irish victims of the escalating famine. On the other hand, the government purchased a large amount of Indian corn and meal from the United States, which was sold at cost to local committees and then sold (at cost) to the poor through food depots since the government did not favor the distribution of food for free.

Still, the scale of the catastrophe in Ireland compelled the British to do something, such as introducing large public works projects that hired destitute men and women in exchange for wages too low to feed a family suffering from starvation. Once the failure of the public works model was recognized, the government opened free soup kitchens, but quickly shut them down despite the fact that they represented the most successful program undertaken by the government during the famine years. From 1847 on, the British preferred the expansion of the workhouse system, in which poor people could work eight to ten hours per day on tasks such as breaking rocks in exchange for food. The workhouses had been crowded before the Great Famine. But, once it had begun, they were filled to triple capacity or more with starving people in no condition for hard labor. Disease in these overcrowded workhouses was rampant and death rates extremely high. Some men and women on the verge of death entered the workhouses only to ensure that they would receive a coffin and a burial. This was far from a viable solution to a crisis of such magnitude, especially when coming from the government of what was then the richest and most powerful nation in the world.

Even more barbaric, while the Irish masses starved to death, a British "poor law" gave landlords a financial incentive to evict destitute families from their tiny plots of land and destroy their houses. As a result, starving people were turned out of their homes and forced to slowly die in the streets as they begged for food. Evictions were carried out by hired men known as the "crowbar brigade," who tore down the mud cabins in which the poor lived, while police stood guard to ensure that the poor didn't actually fight back. Between 1849 and 1854, roughly a quarter of a million people were evicted. The British elite, who viewed the Irish as a lesser form of life, considered all of this to be God's will; a divine punishment of a supposedly backward people. This belief, together with a commitment to laissez-faire economic policies, meant that large-scale famine relief was not forthcoming from Britain.

While Irish emigrants had been heading to the United States in large numbers since Ireland's economy went into decline in 1815, emigration exploded during the Great Famine years. The 1.5 million who left exceeded the number that had departed during the previous twenty-five years. Yet these migrants were not the poorest of the poor, given that the most destitute victims of the famine would not have had the resources necessary to afford the cost of passage on a ship. More than half of famine migrants were unskilled laborers. Up to 90 percent were Catholic, whereas most pre-Famine Irish migrants were Protestant. Very few had any intention of returning to Ireland. Many Irish men and women were persuaded to migrate by the letters they received from friends and family members who had already made the journey. Since many Irish were illiterate, such letters were often read aloud by a local "scholar"—frequently the parish priest.

The night before the intending migrant was to leave, his or her friends and relatives would hold an "American wake," which was devoted to mourning the soon-to-be departed migrant. After a full night of playing music, singing, dancing, eating, and drinking heavily, everyone would accompany the migrant to the train station, or to a nearby crossroads, before the migrant set out on his or her own. Frequently, once the migrant secured work in the United States (or wherever else he or she was going: Great Britain, Canada, Australia), remittances were sent back home to help support the family and relatives were brought over to join the migrant as soon as feasible.

The trip across the Atlantic was grim. It took five or six weeks and often involved badly built ships known as "coffin ships" because they were such death traps. Little food or water was provided, overcrowding was horrendous, and diseases like typhus spread easily throughout the mass of migrants trying to escape the starvation and disease of the Great

The Irish Remedy—Emigration to America
ART AND PICTURE COLLECTION, THE NEW YORK PUBLIC LIBRARY. "THE IRISH REMEDY—EMIGRATION
TO AMERICA." NEW YORK PUBLIC LIBRARY DIGITAL COLLECTIONS. ACCESSED DECEMBER 4, 2017.
HTTP://DIGITALCOLLECTIONS.NYPL.ORG/ITEMS/510D47E1-37DA-A3D9-E040-E00A18064A99

Famine. They died by the tens of thousands. But this did not serve as a deterrent for others seeking a way out of Ireland. In fact, migration remained high even after the Great Famine years. From 1851 to 1921, 4.5 million Irish left their homeland, 3.7 million of whom went to the United States. Most were under the age of thirty, unmarried, and evenly divided between men and women. But at least by the 1860s the coffin ships were a thing of the past; replaced by large steamships that made the voyage in a couple of weeks or less and, thanks to the implementation of new laws, were less crowded and had better food.

Most migrants—Irish or otherwise—passed through New York, and more than a few settled there as well. Migration was a chaotic, unregulated process in which scam artists preyed on new arrivals the minute they stepped off the boat. But the federal government and the governor of New York began to control the process in the 1850s. In 1855, an arrival station was fashioned from a one-time concert hall, Castle Garden, at the tip of Manhattan. There, immigrants could register with U.S. authorities and arrange for a place to stay or transportation for the next leg of their journey. A new immigrant arrival station was opened on Ellis Island in 1892. The first person to arrive at Ellis Island was a fifteen-year-old Irish immigrant named Annie Moore.

Most Irish immigrants were concentrated on the East Coast from Boston to Baltimore, though New York has long been destination number one. In 1860, one-quarter of all New Yorkers were Irish. Though relatively unskilled, the young men and women who immigrated to the United States became a leading force in the city's labor movement, as well as city politics, while remaining staunch supporters of Ireland's independence from Britain.

THE LIONS

León is a big industrial city that is home to about as many people as Dallas, Texas. However, it is not a land of great opportunity. For a working-class man in León, there are two main choices when it comes time to get a job: barely eke out a living in auto repair, the construction trades, or industry—or head north as an undocumented immigrant to the United States, where wages are higher. Anthropologist Ruth Gomberg-Muñoz explores these dual themes in her description of a group of young men she calls the "Lions"—a network of Mexican friends who came from León to work (without papers) in Chicago-area restaurants.[9] As she describes it, staying at home was perceived by the Lions to be a dead end. Most of the Lions' fathers worked in leather manufacturing, shoebox making, or as machinists—sixty hours a week for $200. The Lions' mothers and sisters worked at home selling cosmetics, stationary, or homemade food. The combined income from these endeavors got you a small house and the basic necessities of life, provided that no one got sick or otherwise became unable to work. But even if everyone was busy earning money, things like savings, computers, new clothes, and homes with more than one bedroom were probably out of reach. And this is precisely why so many families depended upon the money sent home by relatives working in the United States (remittances).

What motivated these men to journey to Chicago, and what kept them rooted in León, is succinctly explained by Maria; a mother to two of the Lions. Naturally, she worried about her sons, both of whom were busboys in Chicago. But she was also quite proud of them. Thanks to the money they sent back home, not only did the family have modern appliances, but all three daughters in the family had access to more education than they would have had otherwise. One daughter was a certified public accountant, another had a degree in psychology, and another was beginning a hospitality program to qualify as a manager for high-end hotels in the tourist zones of Mexico.

As this example illustrates, taking the dangerous step of heading across the U.S.-Mexico border without a visa is usually not a decision made by a single individual; it is a family affair. Among the Lions, whoever went to the United States carried a heavy burden since the family back in Mexico would depend upon the flow of remittances in order to meet daily living expenses, buy homes, and pay for the education of other children. Unmarried workers sent a large part of their earnings back home, with roughly half being used for family expenses and the other half saved if a worker planned to buy a house or start a business when he returned to Mexico. When workers got married, more of their money went to their new families and less to their parents.

There were a number of economic factors beyond simple wage differences which made work in the United States so appealing compared to work in Mexico. To begin with, there was the exchange rate. At the time Gomberg-Muñoz was writing, a Mexican peso had about one-tenth the value of a U.S. dollar. So a hundred dollars earned in the United States was magnified enormously in value when sent back to Mexico. Aside from wages and their value, there was also the fact that wage-and-hour laws were more routinely enforced in the United States than in Mexico. A standard work day in the United States was likely to hover close to eight hours (although there were egregious exceptions, to be sure). But in Mexico, workers might be expected to work twelve hours per day, plus six to eight hours on Saturday. Last, though not least, there was relatively widespread access to credit and mortgage markets in the United States, which put car and home ownership within reach of many working-class

Americans. Working-class Mexicans, on the other hand, had little hope of buying a car or home unless they could save a large sum of money—by setting aside a portion of remittances from a son or daughter working in the United States, for instance.

One of the Lions described how he worked in Mexico making shoe boxes; a job that enabled him to pay his bills, but which entailed living paycheck to paycheck with little margin of error. If one of his children became sick and needed to see a doctor, or if the water bill, electric bill, and rent all came due during the same week, he had a serious problem. And so he "jumped the border" to work in Chicago for a while, then went back home with what he had saved. But he kept returning to Chicago to work because the pay was too good to pass up compared to what he made at home. And the longer he stayed in Mexico, the worse his financial situation became, until he was right back where he had started.

There was also a strong social incentive to migrate north, at least for a while: heightened status and prestige back home. While undocumented immigrants have often been demonized in U.S. political rhetoric, they were regarded in Mexico as risk takers who not only wanted more for themselves, but were willing to do what it took to support the family members they left behind. This high degree of motivation was often recognized by the employers who hired undocumented workers once they made it to the United States. It was also frequently recognized by their U.S.-born coworkers, many of whom developed a great deal of respect for the work ethic and sense of family that their undocumented colleagues commonly possessed.

Of course, the plans that undocumented immigrants initially formulate about returning home to Mexico after a period of work in the United States sometimes change. After a while, the United States may become more like "home" than Mexico. This is especially true if many of one's friends and family have also moved to the United States. In some towns in Mexico, for instance, all of the younger men have headed north, leaving behind the women, children, and elderly adults, all of whom are supported by remittances. Or, as sometimes happens, an immigrant meets someone in the United States and falls in love. At that point all future plans must be reevaluated. Nevertheless, there are those undocumented immigrants who do return home after several years of working (and saving) in the United States. And these people are often content with their decision. As one man told Gomberg-Muñoz, he returned to Mexico and stayed because he viewed the quality of life in Mexico as superior to that of the United States, where so much of living revolved around going further into debt in order to acquire more things.

However, this distinction between Mexico and the United States should not be thought of as the difference between a so-called "underdeveloped" country and a "developed" one. The kind of large-scale transnational migration of workers of which the Lions are a part is a symptom of economic development, not its absence. As Mexico has been pulled more and more into the global capitalist system over the decades, inequality has risen and large segments of the Mexican population have lost out. Many Mexican farmers and craft producers have been driven out of business as cheap U.S. imports flood the Mexican market. The rise of the service sector of the U.S. economy has drawn these displaced Mexican farmers and artisans northward and into the United States. Because free-trade agreements between the two countries liberalized trade without liberalizing the flow of workers, these displaced Mexicans have entered without papers. As a result, U.S. border-enforcement policies are undermined by the very economic policies that have been favored for so long by U.S. politicians and the business community.

Still, border enforcement is a deadly serious business. When each of the Lions decided to cross the border into the United States even once—let alone multiple times back and forth, as some did—they assumed a level of risk that should not be underestimated. Anyone trying to make it across the border while staying under the radar can easily die along the way of heat stroke, dehydration, hypothermia, or drowning; be shot by an immigration agent, police officer, property owner, border vigilante, drug smuggler, or gang member; be raped, robbed, or abandoned in the desert by a coyote (people smuggler). This is why, from fiscal year 1998 to fiscal year 2013, the U.S. Border Patrol estimates that 6,029 migrants died on the U.S. side of the U.S.-Mexico border while trying to enter the United States.[10] This is not the kind of trip anyone would undertake lightly.

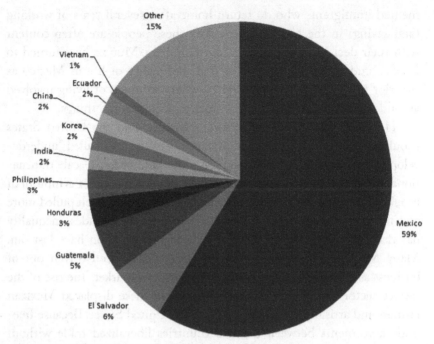

Unauthorized Population by Country of Origin, 2012
SOURCE: BRYAN BAKER AND NANCY RYTINA, ESTIMATES OF THE UNAUTHORIZED IMMIGRANT POP-ULATION RESIDING IN THE UNITED STATES: JANUARY 2012 (WASHINGTON, DC: U.S. DEPARTMENT OF HOMELAND SECURITY, OFFICE OF IMMIGRATION STATISTICS, MARCH 2013), P. 5.

Nor should the cost of hiring a coyote as a guide into the United States be taken lightly. As U.S. border-enforcement tactics make it increasingly difficult to get across the border, the price of doing so keeps going up and now amounts to a few thousand dollars. Since the average working-class Mexican does not have that kind of money lying around, it is necessary to get a "sponsor"—a family member or close friend already in the United States who can front that kind of cash. All of the Lions had done this for at least one family member or friend. The newly sponsored arrival had to work as hard as possible to repay that loan, or risk becoming an outcast from the social network that made his or her journey possible. Someone wouldn't risk both death and debt without being serious about getting ahead in the United States.

CHAPTER THREE

The Ladder of Success

It is undeniable that the forces of globalization have uprooted millions upon millions of migratory laborers with relatively low levels of formal education and training who make their way to the United States to fill low-wage jobs. But that is only part of the story. There are—and have long been—highly skilled immigrants as well; immigrants whose specialized knowledge, at one time, earned them relatively high incomes and social status. However, poor (or deteriorating) economic conditions in their home countries motivated them to seek out better opportunities in the United States. For instance, before the influx of displaced Italian peasants at the end of the nineteenth century, the United States had become home to thousands of professionals and artisans from Italy. Similarly, many of the Russian Jews who immigrated to the United States in the eighteen hundreds were skilled industrial workers in the needle trades.[1]

Nevertheless, it wasn't until the 1970s that the U.S. economy began to generate a high demand for immigrants with advanced degrees who could fill highly skilled positions. This shift in labor demand reflected a twofold transformation in the U.S. economy. First, technological innovation increased the ease and speed of both communication and transportation, which meant that products could be made in one part of the world and sold in another with minimal cost and hassle. Second, increased economic competition from other countries (Japan, in particular) spurred many U.S. companies to relocate their production facilities to other countries where costs were lower (meaning, primarily, that workers could be paid less than in the United States). As a result, the manufacturing sector of the U.S. economy dried up, being either offshored or driven out of the market by other companies. With U.S. manufacturing jobs disappearing, what remained were a growing number of low-end service jobs and high-end professional and technical jobs. This split between less-skilled and high-skilled jobs, with relatively few jobs falling in between, created a growing demand for both less-educated and highly educated immigrant workers.[2]

At the dawn of the twenty-first century, the U.S. economy had an appetite for immigrant labor that seemed to be insatiable. As sociologists Wayne Cornelius, Thomas Espenshade, and Margaret Usdansky describe it, the front door of the United States was open to foreign workers with advanced degrees, meaning that work visas were available for at least a sizeable chunk of the immigrants who wanted to come.[3] For workers without a high-school diploma, on the other hand, the nation's back door was open. That is to say, they were able to enter without official permission and work in an undocumented status—always at risk of detention and deportation, particularly if they had any run-ins with the police.

Just as the presence of less-educated immigrants in the U.S. labor force sparked endless debates over whether or not immigrants were "stealing" less-skilled jobs from native-born Americans with little schooling, so too did the presence of immigrants with high-tech skills provoke arguments over the displacement of American engineers and computer programmers. But this was by no means the first public debate over the merits and drawbacks of high-skilled immigration. More than a century ago, in the 1880s, after laws had been passed banning the immigration of contract workers, loopholes in those laws allowed foreign workers of various skill levels to come to the United States, from domestic servants to artists, lecturers, and actors. In 1891, exemptions were also created for professors, ministers, and all others with a "recognized profession." Even the draconian national-origin quotas created in 1924 exempted some ministers and college professors from abroad—as long as they weren't Asians, who were categorically excluded.

The importance of labor qualifications in gaining entry to the United States was even evident in how the United States approached the immense number of refugees created by the carnage of World War II. In the late 1940s, as laws were being passed to admit hundreds of thousands of European refugees into the United States, preference was given to both agricultural workers and to professionals and technical workers. This growing tendency to take education and skills into account when admitting immigrants into the country continued, with the 1952 McCarran-Walter Act giving preference to immigrants with skills and knowledge deemed by the attorney general as serving important U.S. interests. Despite these preferences, the numbers of high-skilled immigrants coming to the United States never exceeded a few thousand per year during the 1950s.

Beginning in 1965, when the national-origin quota system was dismantled and replaced, opportunities for skilled migration expanded considerably. Although 80 percent of visas under the new system were reserved for immigrants with family ties to the United States, the remaining 20 percent were allocated to employment-based immigration (both high-skilled and less-skilled). Not surprisingly, labor unions worried that immigrants who came to the United States through employment-based channels would be used by employers to drive down wages and take jobs from native-born workers. In response to these concerns, the new system included a requirement that the immigrants work only in occupations certified by the secretary of labor as experiencing labor shortages, and that the wages and working conditions of native-born workers would not deteriorate due to the presence of immigrant workers.

The next big change in the world of high-skilled immigration was the Immigration Act of 1990, which dramatically increased the number of employment-based visas in general and visas for high-skilled immigrants in particular. The law sought to address some of the major complaints about the inadequacies of the system created in 1965. For instance, employers said the old regime didn't give them the workers they needed, while labor unions said it let in foreign workers on high-skilled visas who really weren't high-skilled. In response, the 1990 law created new legal avenues for immigration by both permanent and temporary high-skilled workers—ostensibly with more rigorous standards as well as more protections built in for native-born workers than had previously existed. For temporary workers, for instance, a new H-1B visa was created in response to employer demand for high-skilled labor, but it required employers to pay foreign workers the "prevailing wage" in their occupation to ensure that H-1B visa recipients wouldn't be used to undercut wages for native-born workers. The number of new H-1Bs available for any given year was determined by congressional negotiations.

But in the midst of modern debates over skill levels and labor shortages, it's important to keep in mind that skilled immigrants have been part of the U.S. economy for much of the nation's history. Long before immigrants from India were feeding the science and engineering workforce of Silicon Valley, skilled craftsmen from Germany were escaping the wrenching political and economic transformations in their homeland in favor of the relative political stability and economic opportunity of the United States.

THE ARTISANS

It would be hard to overestimate the impact that immigration had on U.S. society in the period leading up to the Civil War. Between 1840 and 1860, more than four million immigrants arrived, which amounted to roughly 30 percent of the "free" (non-slave) population as of 1840. Three-quarters came from Germany or Ireland. As historian Bruce Levine notes, immigrants were half the population in Chicago and 40 percent in New York.[4] Most immigrants entered the nascent industrial working class of the United States, but many entered professional occupations. A few joined the economic upper class.

Many Americans have forgotten about the history of German immigration to the United States, but there was a time when Germans predominated. During the 1850s, nine out of ten European immigrants came from Germany. Given their numbers, German immigrants were a driving force in labor unions. And many—both intellectuals and laborers—were political exiles who brought with them the ideals of Germany's 1848 revolution. Their sentiments frequently fed into the anti-slavery movement which culminated in the Civil War.

Most German immigrants were peasants, artisans, and laborers. They were motivated to leave Germany by both rapid industrialization

From the Old to the New World—German Emigrants for New York Embarking on a Hamburg Steamer
PUBLISHED 1874, HARPER'S WEEKLY. LC-USZ62-100310

and economic stagnation. Compared to the industrializing British economy, Germany was downright backward in the early nineteenth century. Peasants still labored in the service of hereditary lords. Large portions of German society were feudal; dominated by aristocrats and clergy. The German "nation" was actually a collection of more than three hundred largely independent territories; each with its own tolls, tariffs, and economic monopolies.

However, capitalist industrialization was starting to creep across the country in fits and starts. Wealthy merchants and businesses geared towards profit were appearing. Peasants and artisans who lost their property were forced to sell their labor to agricultural or industrial employers in order to survive. Abject poverty deepened. And craftsmen began to face more and more competition.

At the beginning of the eighteen hundreds, there were 1.1 million primarily middle-class craftsmen who comprised one-tenth of the German labor force, accounting for more than half of the production of nonagricultural goods. They worked with journeymen and apprentices who often lived with them and hoped to one day strike out on their own. But times were changing. At the start of the nineteenth century, about half of craftsmen only employed themselves and sometimes members of their families. They became increasingly dependent on orders from merchants. Gradually, they were becoming more like wage laborers.

Faced with growing economic competition from an increasingly industrialized England, German state bureaucracies instituted reforms to overhaul land ownership, taxation, education, commerce, and select industries in order to strengthen the economy in general and the power of existing elites in particular. For instance, peasants were "liberated" from serfdom, but often ended up losing their land in the process. The end result was more landless peasants, as well as small landowners who were just barely hanging on, to serve as workers in mechanized agriculture. Yet these changes occurred gradually and did not instantly override the old way of doing things. For instance, payment of tribute to hereditary nobles persisted for decades despite the spread of the industrial model.

In the midst of this economic transformation, the German population was growing rapidly—increasing by more than half between 1800 and 1850. The population of rural areas alone grew by nearly ten million. Small landowners squeezed everything they could out of shrinking plots of land and became increasingly reliant on potatoes and turnips to feed themselves. In fact, root vegetables jumped from being three percent of the Prussian harvest in 1800 to one-quarter by 1840. All of this translated into a massive surplus of rural workers who were driven by necessity into various cottage industries, as well as into factories. And some migrated abroad.

During this period, the German transportation system grew enormously, amounting to hundreds or even thousands of miles in new railway tracks, canals, and roads. Mechanization gradually took hold in a wide range of industries, from textiles to baked goods. Yet even by the 1850s, mechanization was not the norm throughout Germany. Nor were centralized industries with significant division of labor among workers. Most production was done with traditional hand tools on a very small scale.

Within the production of handicrafts, an increasing number of journeymen and apprentices were dependent for their livelihoods on a declining group of small masters. The shops of the masters gradually began to produce just a few goods that sold well rather than a wide range of products. In contrast to the old days, journeymen were no longer part of the master's family, but were treated like wage-earning workers required to labor for up to fourteen hours per day for a meager sum of money. Masters became increasingly concerned with profit and competition from British and German factories. Many masters were masters in name only; bearing the title but lacking the independence and the capital to back it up. Some were poverty stricken themselves and saddled with loans that carried interest rates of 10–20 percent.

The European potato blight of 1845 wiped out German peasants and agricultural laborers and contributed to food shortages aggravated by poor grain harvests. When a financial crisis also hit in 1847–1848, food prices rose and many peasants reduced their purchases from craftsmen, who often went bankrupt as a result. Hunger riots erupted in cities and towns around the country. Craftworkers without work fought government troops and in some cases attacked factories and destroyed the machinery inside. In short, a revolutionary situation was in the making.

The German revolution derived much inspiration from events in France, where the monarchy collapsed and was replaced with a new form of government in 1848. German aristocrats tried to defuse the situation by appointing their critics to government ministries, but the mood of the German people remained volatile. They battled with government troops in the streets of Berlin, leaving many dead. Skilled craftworkers made up two-thirds of the dead—including masters, journeymen, and apprentices who had worked as cabinetmakers, tailors, shoemakers, locksmiths, blacksmiths, silk weavers, bookbinders, carpenters, and masons. Some revolutionaries wanted liberal democracy, others socialism. Journeymen printers called the first national strike in German history in 1848.

At the same time that turmoil and hardship were engulfing Germany, travelers' accounts and personal letters portrayed the United States as a sort of paradise in which land and jobs were available in abundance. So a growing number of Germans began migrating there. While the stories of plenty were greatly exaggerated, the U.S. economy was far more dynamic and rapidly growing than the German economy. Few German immigrants had the kind of capital needed to start farming (start-up costs for a small farmer were estimated at between $750 and $1,550). So most Germans congregated in towns and cities. Three-quarters of German immigrants in 1860 lived in nine mid-Atlantic and Midwestern states (New York, New Jersey, Pennsylvania, Ohio, Illinois, Wisconsin, Indiana, Michigan, and Iowa). At the top of the German American social hierarchy were wealthy merchants, financiers, and manufacturing employers with extensive business ties in Germany. Next were medium and large-scale entrepreneurs (merchants, manufacturers, owners of big hotels and restaurants), and professionals (doctors, lawyers, clergy, journalists). At the bottom, as always, was the working-class majority. Former peasants usually ended up in less-skilled jobs such as longshoreman, porter, domestic servant, and laborer.

A considerable number of German craftsmen resumed their trades. The 1870 census found a disproportionate number of Germans working in clothes production, carpentry, furniture making, boot and shoemaking, blacksmithing, butchering, baking, masonry, plastering, and cigar-making. While Germans were one out of every twenty-three inhabitants of the United States, they were nearly 40 percent of all bakers, nearly one-third of butchers, more than one in four cabinetmakers, one in five clothing workers, one in six boot and shoemakers, and one in eight tanners, leather finishers, saddle and harness makers, and masons.

Nearly one in 10 Germans in the country lived in New York, where they comprised 15 percent of the city's population and 22 percent of the workforce. More than half of the employed Germans were craftworkers, particularly in the garment industry, shoe manufacture, and furniture making. In short, Germans were major players in the principal sectors of the manufacturing economy as it existed in the mid-nineteenth century. Some of the most highly skilled artisans garnered high incomes making jewelry, clothes, boots and shoes, furniture, ornamental ironwork, coaches, and carriages on a limited quantity, made-to-order basis. But even craftsmen outside of the luxury markets could do well; as house carpenters, for instance.

Life as an immigrant craftsman from Germany was not all wine and roses, however. As most visitors from Europe quickly noticed, the pace of work in the United States was much faster than in the old country. Immigrant workers of all varieties had to learn to keep up if they were going to make it. And making it in the U.S. economy was not as easy as the stories back in Germany made it sound. In fact, artisans were gradually giving way to wage laborers. But this was not a clear-cut process. It usually involved moving from independent production to increasing degrees of dependence on merchants and subcontractors. As early as the 1850s, cabinetmakers in the Midwest were taking jobs in large factories with steam-powered equipment. Yet many independent cabinetmaking shops coexisted with the factories.

In addition to the slow progression of industrialization, German immigrant craftworkers found in the United States the cold cruelty of the business cycle. While 1843–1854 was a period of economic growth and rising employment, it brought with it inflation that ate away at wages and lowered living standards—especially after the discovery of gold in California in 1848. The economy faltered at the end of 1854, began to recover from 1855 to 1856, then collapsed in 1857. Unemployment skyrocketed. From the perspective of many German immigrants, the United States was beginning to look very much like the old country. And with the rise of economic hardship, U.S. society became more xenophobic.

Still, true to the spirit that inspired Germany's 1848 revolution, German immigrants played pivotal roles in some of the key labor mobilizations of the 1850s, such as the 1850 tailors' strike. And the spirit of 1848 motivated a great many German immigrants—although by no means all—to oppose slavery in the run up to the Civil War. They may not have been able to preserve their old livelihoods in the face of the Industrial Revolution—few Americans could—but German immigrants did make their presence felt throughout U.S. society.

THE TECHIES

The stereotype of the Indian immigrant with a knowledge of all things high-tech is by now familiar to many Americans. But, as scholars such as Paula Chakravartty and Roli Varma explain, the historical reality that lies beneath that stereotype is complex.[5] To start with, the first immigrants from India tended to be relatively unskilled. They were primarily lone men, without wives or children in tow, who worked as laborers building railroads, bridges, and tunnels, or as field hands on California farms, in the latter half of the nineteenth century. Although they were few in number, there were enough to provoke the ire of America nativists. They were forbidden to own land, marry whites, or live in certain areas. And on September 5, 1907, white mobs took things a step further and drove Indian workers out of Bellingham, Washington. The Asian Exclusion League targeted Indians in a more methodical fashion, persuading the federal government to restrict Indian immigration—which hardly seemed necessary considering that many Indians were voluntarily leaving the country in response to persistent harassment and violence. To justify these actions, nativists trotted out the usual clichés, claiming that Indians stole jobs from white men, didn't assimilate, carried diseases, and were repositories for all sorts of undesirable personality traits, like lustfulness and insolence.

Unfortunately, most U.S. lawmakers of the time found such stereotypes persuasive. And so, in 1917, immigration by Indians wasn't just subjected to further restrictions, it was completely shut down by the Barred Zone Act, which also closed the door to all other Asians. In the wake of this law, Indians already in the United States kept a low profile. Many gave up their turbans in order to "pass" as black or Mexican, which was widely perceived to be a step up from Indian. As of 1940, nearly half of Indians in this country were farm laborers and over one-third had not finished even one year of school.

It wasn't until 1946 that a handful of Indian immigrants were once again allowed to enter the United States, and Indians already living here were allowed to apply for U.S. citizenship (a reward to India for supporting the United States in World War II). In a break with the past, most of these new immigrants were professionals who brought their families with them. Although this was a reversal of previous patterns, it was not that surprising given the nature of Indian society. During the colonial period, Britain created a number of English-language schools, colleges, and universities in India that followed strictly Western models of education. After independence in 1947, India retained that system of education and therefore produced rather large numbers of highly educated workers; at the same time much of the poor majority remained illiterate. This represented a conscious choice by government officials to invest far more in higher education than in basic literacy and elementary education in order to rapidly create skilled professionals who could build the high-tech sectors viewed as crucial to India's economic development. From roughly 1950 to 1980, these sectors were identified by the government as aerospace, nuclear power, and electronics.

However, the flow of Indian professionals into the United States could not begin in earnest until the 1965 Immigration and Nationality Act lifted racist national quotas in favor of a uniform limit of twenty thousand per country (at least in the Eastern Hemisphere), and emphasized the entrance of immigrants who could serve U.S. economic needs. Indian immigration rose dramatically. By 1990, there would be more than eight hundred fifteen thousand Indian immigrants in the United States. Most came as foreign students to earn graduate degrees in science or engineering, after which they frequently became lawful permanent residents (LPRs) and stayed. Of course, the United States wouldn't be such an appealing option for Indian students if not for the fact that their respective educational systems are compatible. Indians attending U.S. universities find themselves on relatively familiar ground, with Western-style classes taught in English. It is also worth noting that, in the decades after the end of World War II, a new, more positive stereotype of Indian immigrants emerged. Now they were often seen as naturally intelligent and hardworking high achievers.

The 1990s was a pivotal decade in the development of India's high-tech industries, as well as in the flow of Indian professionals to the countries of the so-called "developed" world, like the United States. As the decade began, India faced a severe economic crisis and had little choice but to do as the International Monetary Fund and the World Bank demanded, which was to open the economy to international competition. As the market rather than the Indian state was permitted to guide the country's investment decisions, computers and software came to be the newest, hottest commodities. At the same time, international competition was intense for dominance in a variety of high-tech industries, leading the United States, Europe, and Japan to vie with each other for the world's highly skilled workers who were needed to run those industries. Since India had a large pool of skilled workers, but a relatively small domestic market for computer services (poor people didn't have computers), software was produced primarily for export. During this period, Bangalore became recognized as the Silicon Valley of India. Moreover, companies like Cisco, Ford, and IBM began setting up research and development operations in India, taking advantage of highly trained Indian workers who labored for much lower pay than a U.S. worker.

While India carved out a niche for itself in the global IT market, it was not the niche that the nation's elites had expected. Despite a high-end beginning in software development, India's IT industry became a global player in low-end code writing. Moreover, most of the export revenue generated by the Indian IT sector eventually came not from product development, but from services performed by "information workers." These outsourced workers were either hired by transnational corporations that set up shop in India, or worked outside of the country on short-term contracts—a practice which came to be known, rather crudely but accurately, as "body shopping."

One way in which the United States sought out a bigger cut of the global labor pool so necessary for a high-tech economy was by creating, in 1990, the H-1B visa for highly skilled professionals—which became an avenue into the country for many Indian workers. During the 1990s, Indians received about half of all H-1Bs. The immediate justification for this visa was that U.S. industries were experiencing shortages of high-skilled workers, in part because U.S. universities weren't graduating enough native-born students with science or engineering degrees.

The Indian scientists and engineers (and science and engineering students) who responded to this demand didn't immigrate to the United States simply because salaries were higher. Many Indian scientists and engineers earned good salaries in India and were quite content to live there. Yet some who were living relatively comfortable lives chose to uproot themselves and move to the United States for a new job or to pursue a graduate degree. Two of the most commonly cited reasons for doing so were greater educational opportunities, particularly at the graduate level, and a wider range of career choices. An undergraduate degree from the Indian Institute of Technology was internationally competitive. But options within India for graduate education in many specialized fields, let alone jobs in many specialized fields, were more limited—hence the decision to migrate. Nevertheless, even with these improved opportunities, most Indian scientists and engineers ran up against a "silicon ceiling" when it came to entering the ranks of upper management in the companies where they worked. It is telling that most of the Indian chief executive officers (CEOs) of high-tech companies were leading companies they founded or cofounded, like Sabeer Bhatia of Hotmail, Vinod Khosla of Sun Microsystems, and Vivek Wadhwa of Relativity Technologies.

At first, the emigration of highly skilled workers from India was seen as an example of "brain drain" that robbed the Indian economy of its best and brightest professionals to the benefit of the economies of the United States, the United Kingdom, and Canada. However, the notion of "brain drain" assumes that migrants, as well as their economic and intellectual power, are forever lost to India and that emigration is permanent. In reality, as the practice of body shopping illustrates, emigration is not necessarily a one-way street. Even though relatively few high-tech Indian immigrants returned to India for good, they sent remittances and potentially valuable knowledge to their family members still in India, and they traveled back and forth between the two countries. That is why, in 1975, the Indian government created the category of "non-resident Indian" (NRI), and allowed NRIs to open foreign-currency bank accounts in India. Many Indian scientists and engineers who immigrated to the United States and chose to remain there did so primarily because of the family connections they had developed, particularly having children for whom the United States was home. And there was the fact that India had an overabundance of high-tech graduates compared to the number of decent jobs that were available. In addition, Indian immigrants to the United States who decided to stay knew that they could regularly visit family and friends back in India without much trouble.

It was in this economic milieu that U.S. NRIs played a major role in the development of the high-tech economy in India. They acted as brokers, both economic and cultural, when it came to body shopping contracts and the opening of India to offshore software operations owned by transnational corporations. Microsoft and IBM were just two of the IT behemoths that opened academic training programs through established Indian universities and technical colleges in order to train future crops of high-tech Indian workers. While some Indians viewed NRIs as heroes for contributing to India's economic development, others saw them as complicit in a colonial enterprise. In this view, foreign corporations were not investing in the development of a robust IT sector in India. They were investing in the training of low-end tech workers who would help those corporations develop high-end software that could then be sold back to India at a profit. As one Indian executive described it, "We are exporting cotton and buying back the finished cloth."

Regardless of its economic or ethical merits, the transnational IT industry was much sought after throughout India. States and cities competed with each other for the favors of transnational IT corporations, designating locales as "techno-parks" and "high-tech cities." Not only IBM and Microsoft came; 3M, General Electric, Hewlett-Packard, Oracle, Texas Instruments, and Sun Microsystems also had a presence in India. Meanwhile, Indian H-1B holders were often well paid in Silicon Valley and elsewhere in the United States. And there were NRI executives based in Silicon Valley who created startups in India.

All of this economic activity notwithstanding, most new jobs were in basic programming and data processing. Plus, more recently, new jobs were being created by the "virtual" outsourcing of information-age functions like customer support, mail-order services, medical transcription, telephone operations, and airline reservations. That is, satellite links and fiber-optic lines allowed workers based in India to perform these tasks for any group of consumers anywhere in the world. NRI entrepreneurs were players in this relatively new realm, with their basic pitch to customers or investors being that Indian workers would be willing to do the same job for less pay than comparable workers in the United States.

However, not all Indians were satisfied with the economic direction of the nation. Social groups that had historically been left out of India's economic successes were now politically active, and didn't necessarily agree with the path of liberalization favored by American NRIs and other business leaders. Hence, the frequent national elections, fragile coalition governments, and regular demonstrations and strikes that came to characterize modern India—these were political manifestations not only of differences in class, but caste and region as well. This was the political environment within which transnational corporations and their local affiliates operated.

Political instability notwithstanding, the Indian state encouraged Indian students to migrate abroad, particularly to the United States, in order to gain a valuable high-tech education, and then come back home with their knowledge and freshly acquired entrepreneurial zeal. The entrepreneurship of these return migrants was seen as a key ingredient in healthy political and trade relations between India and the United States. In fact, Indians were frequently portrayed as naturals in high-tech endeavors because of some supposed Hindu capitalist predilection for the intricacies of coding and the internet economy.[6] Such stereotypes were inherently racist, even if they did carry a positive spin, and were based more on imagination than reality. For instance, the common claim that Indian students were so good at grasping science and technology because they had parents who stressed those fields didn't quite square with the fact that half of India's population was illiterate. Seen in this light, it might be argued that NRIs benefited more from being privileged than from being Indian.

Regardless of the reasons for their success, Indian scientists and engineers in the United States were now part of a diaspora; a transnational network of high-tech students and professionals, and their family members, who circulated between two continents. Some came to earn a PhD and then return for good to India. Others stayed in the United States for the rest of their lives to work in professional positions, while traveling regularly back to India. And others divided their work lives between the United States and India, perhaps working for many years in a high-powered job in the United States, then moving back to India to assume a comparable—or even better—job there. The end result was a continual movement of people, knowledge, and money that tied both countries together.

PART 2

HOMECOMINGS

Chapter Four

Pieces of Paper

THE LEGAL RIGHTS THAT IMMIGRANTS HAVE IN THE UNITED STATES, and the legal dangers they face, depend in large part on what official documents (or "papers") they possess. If they are undocumented, in which case they probably have fake identification documents or authentic documents that belong to someone else, then their rights are few and they can be detained and deported at any moment if they end up in the hands of federal immigration agents. If the immigrants in question are lawful permanent residents ("green card" holders), they are not in as much legal peril as the undocumented, but they still face a fair amount of risk. A green card certainly signifies that an immigrant is here legally, but it also means that the immigrant is ruled by a second-rate system of justice which can expel him or her from the country for even a minor brush with the law. For instance, a green card holder who pled guilty to possession of marijuana in 2000 and served no jail time will likely be deported the next time he or she has any contact with the immigration system. On paper, at least, the only immigrants who have the same rights as native-born U.S. citizens are those who have become naturalized U.S. citizens.

The U.S. deportation machine has been running on high gear for quite some time. Even during the ostensibly liberal administration of President Barack Obama, federal immigration authorities carried out somewhere in the neighborhood of three million removals from the United States (a figure which includes an unknown number of multiple removals of the same individual).[1] Supporters of the mass deportation system claim that these removals enhanced public safety by taking dangerous criminals off the street, but this is far from the truth. Although dangerous criminals were no doubt among those immigrants removed, the overwhelming majority were undocumented immigrants and green card holders guilty of minor infractions. In the United States, deportation isn't primarily about public safety or crime fighting; it's about social control. That is to say, it's the selective exercise of state power over particular groups of people.

SOCIAL CONTROL

The U.S. deportation system exerts control over different groups of people in different ways.[2] It mandates the expulsion of those who have entered the country either by evading border controls or misrepresenting who they were. It calls for the removal of those who fail to live up to the terms of their visa (like a foreign student who doesn't maintain a full course load). And it places even legal immigrants on a period of indefinite probation, although they are never informed of this fact. What this means is that even a long-term green card holder must always be on his or her best behavior, lest a seemingly inconsequential run-in with the law trigger automatic deportation.

One important aspect of the deportation system is how few rights it accords deportees in comparison to defendants in criminal proceedings. Deportees will not be read their Miranda rights. They may not be told that they have the right to an attorney, and none will be provided if they can't afford one. They will not have a right to a trial by jury. They may have to prove that they aren't guilty of some offense, rather than the federal government being obligated to prove that they are guilty. In short, a deportee often has little more than the right to show up for a proceeding and listen to what the government has already decided to do.

This system, in which the deck is so effectively stacked against anyone who is not a U.S. citizen, has been a long time in the making. As legal scholar Daniel Kanstroom explains, although societies and social groups have always distinguished between "us" and "them," the first U.S. experiment in the formulation of a deportation law came with the Alien and Sedition Acts of 1798. At the time, war with France seemed to be a very real possibility. And so the Federalists, who controlled both houses of

Congress and the presidency, passed laws giving the federal government the explicit authority to prosecute and deport foreigners who were citizens of a hostile power—in this case, of course, France—or any noncitizen deemed by the president to be a threat to the United States, for that matter. The laws also went a step further and restricted anti-government speech by anyone—citizen or non-citizen. However, with the Federalists beginning a downward spiral towards extinction shortly thereafter, these laws were enforced for only a little while. At the time the laws were being debated, Thomas Jefferson famously warned that whatever limitations on basic rights might be applied first to the "friendless alien," those limitations would eventually be applied to U.S. citizens as well.

The colonial mentality of U.S. society provided other justifications for the forcible movement of noncitizens from place to place. For instance, the expulsion of American Indians from their own land was rooted in a presumed right of conquest that was ultimately rooted in the alleged superiority of European "civilizations" over the lesser societies of "savages." Following the Civil War, the U.S. Army and civilian contractors proved their civilized superiority by massacring or deliberately starving thousands of Indian men, women, and children in order to remove them from their lands. In short, Indians may have been here first, but they were treated very much as "aliens." Similarly, before the Civil War, the 1850 Fugitive Slave Act gave slave owners and their agents the right to cross state lines in order to abduct slaves who had escaped from them, and then return these escaped slaves to their captivity. A number of congressmen from (non-slave-owning) northeastern states vigorously opposed this law, but to no avail. A primary justification for this barbaric treatment was that African Americans weren't U.S. citizens, and therefore weren't entitled to constitutional protections.

It wasn't until the end of the nineteenth century that a full-blown exclusion and deportation system was created that targeted a particular group of people: the Chinese, who were first drawn to California by the gold rush of 1849. After a brief honeymoon period of welcome in the United States, Chinese workers were demonized in every conceivable way by native-born whites who were fearful of their presence, yet confident in their own Anglo superiority. In the end, the federal government in 1882 banned the entry of new Chinese immigrants into the country, didn't allow those already in the country to naturalize and become U.S. citizens, and mandated the expulsion of those Chinese immigrants who were found to be present without papers.

In the early nineteen hundreds, new categories were added to the list of offenses worthy of excluding an intending immigrant trying to enter the United States, or deporting an immigrant already here. Not only was being Chinese such an offense; so was being a criminal, anarchist, communist, or striking worker. But, as historian Mae Ngai points out, the truly pivotal year in the development of the U.S. deportation system during the early twentieth century was the creation of the "national origins quota system" in 1924. This marked the first time the U.S. government had imposed numerical restrictions on immigration from every country in the world, with favored racial groups and nationalities receiving higher quotas and unwanted races and nationalities receiving little or no access to the United States.

Thanks in large part to the rise of nationalism (of the white, Protestant variety), the door was closed to southern and eastern Europeans, as well as all Asians and Africans. In the twisted world view of anti-immigration activists, the United States was experiencing "racial indigestion" due to the arrival of so many immigrants belonging to nonwhite races. The pseudo-science of eugenics was all the rage at the time and guided members of Congress as they constructed a racial hierarchy in which only northern and western Europeans came out on top. But it is noteworthy that immigrants from Mexico (and the rest of Latin America) were exempt from numerical limits. This exception was the result of both the foreign policy interests of the U.S. government and the heavy dependence of farmers in western states on Mexican labor—in particular, workers who would come for the harvest season and then go back across the border and stay in Mexico until they were needed again.

In the same way that the exemption of Mexico from quotas was tied to economics, so was the forced reduction of immigration from just about everywhere else. As the U.S. economy became more dependent on technological change and less dependent on large numbers of workers to fill less-skilled jobs, there was no longer the kind of labor demand for Italian and Russian immigrants that had existed at the turn of the century. A racial hierarchy dressed up as science provided a convenient way to shut down the migrant pipeline from those countries.

Even while the racial alchemy of the 1924 law was still running its course, the deportation regime was experiencing other changes. After the Japanese bombing of Pearl Harbor, in 1941, President Franklin D. Roosevelt literally took a page from the 1798 Enemy Aliens Act—which was still on the books—and quickly signed orders authorizing the detention of anyone of Japanese ancestry within the United States. U.S. citizenship provided no protection. By the time World War II ended, more than seventy thousand U.S. citizens, plus forty thousand noncitizens (mostly green card holders), had been uprooted from their homes, shipped off to "relocation centers," and held prisoner for years. Oddly enough, the camps were actually overseen by political liberals who took this mass imprisonment as an opportunity to foster the assimilation of Japanese immigrants into an Anglo version of U.S. culture. Regardless of this benevolent intent, the fact remains that at this historical moment, "aliens" included U.S. citizens and deportations took place within the boundaries of the United States—only the deportees were deposited in a U.S. prison camp, not Japan.

Although these imprisoned Japanese Americans experienced the absolute worst the U.S. deportation system had to offer, Mexicans were not strangers to its brutality. During the 1930s, in the midst of the Great Depression, more than one million people of Mexican ancestry—both immigrants and their native-born children—were forcibly removed from the United States and shipped off to Mexico in an effort to free up jobs for newly unemployed white Americans. Yet the demand for Mexican agricultural workers rose again after the end of the depression. In response, the federal government created the Bracero program, which brought 4.6 million Mexican agricultural workers into the country on a temporary basis between 1942 and 1964.

Not surprisingly, undocumented immigration rose hand-in-hand with the Bracero program. And so, in 1954, the federal government launched Operation Wetback, which rounded up and deported 1.1 million undocumented Mexican workers—often under horrendous conditions.

Congressional investigators likened one of the ships which was used to transport roughly one-quarter of all deportees back to Mexico as similar to an "eighteenth century slave ship." Some deportees were taken across the border by truck or bus and dumped in the desert, where they were left to fend for themselves. On one such occasion, eighty-eight deportees died from sunstroke in 112-degree heat. And more would have died if not for the intervention of the Red Cross. Despite such dramatic actions, white farmers in the Southwest remained heavily dependent on Mexican farmhands—whether they were legal or not. It is telling that, during the lifespan of the Bracero program, the number of agricultural laborers brought in legally from Mexico was nearly the same as the number of undocumented workers deported back to Mexico.

After four long decades, the blatantly racist system of immigration quotas defined by national origin was toppled by the Immigration Act of 1965, which established a global ceiling of two hundred ninety thousand per year on immigration to the United States: one hundred seventy thousand from the Eastern Hemisphere and one hundred twenty thousand from the Western Hemisphere. Each country in the Eastern Hemisphere had an allotment of twenty thousand per year (which at least put Italy and Russia back on an equal footing with England and France), while there were no country-specific quotas for the Western Hemisphere (a reflection of the fact that Mexico and Canada had deep economic and social ties to the United States). Unfortunately, in 1976, the per-country quota of twenty thousand was imposed on the Western Hemisphere as well, which meant that Mexico was now subject to the same numerical cap as, say, Mongolia. This was a recipe for more undocumented immigration, and more deportations. Nevertheless, the 1965 act did manage to dismantle an overtly white-supremacist model of immigration.

A darker chapter in the history of the U.S. deportation system came in 1996 with passage of the Illegal Immigration Reform and Immigrant Responsibility Act (IIRAIRA) and the Antiterrorism and Effective Death Penalty Act (AEDPA). Together, these laws greatly increased the legal perils faced even by immigrants with green cards, who were made deportable for all sorts of nonviolent offenses, no matter how old or how minor those offenses were. Not even the judges hearing the deportation cases were allowed to let "guilty" immigrants stay in the country, regardless of how sympathetic their plight might be.

Mae Ngai tells the story of Rosario Hernandez, a thirty-nine-year-old construction worker in Texas who came to the United States as a teenager. The Immigration and Naturalization Service (INS) ordered that he be deported back to Mexico in 2001 because he had two twenty-year-old drunk driving convictions, and one ten-year-old conviction. He had been sentenced to five weekends in jail, joined Alcoholics Anonymous, and successfully quit drinking. His wife was a U.S. citizen and they had two children who were U.S. citizens. But none of that mattered. He had been deemed guilty of an "aggravated felony" for his offenses and his removal from the country was mandatory under the 1996 laws. There would not even be any judicial review of his case. Instead, he was torn from his home and family and dumped back into a country where he hadn't lived for decades. As Rosario correctly noted, he was being punished twice for the same crime.[3]

THE FIRST ILLEGAL IMMIGRANTS

The first illegal border crossers into the United States were not Mexican, or even Latin American—they were Chinese and Japanese. Historian Erika Lee explains that the reason for this is quite simple: the Chinese and Japanese were the first immigrants to be barred from entering the country.[4] The justifications for excluding them were explicitly racist. Asians were presumed not only to be racially inferior to Anglos, but to pose a racial threat to Anglos as well. The anti-Asian racists of the day relied upon many of the same stereotypes that were used to denigrate African Americans, with both groups presumed to be immoral savages prone to lust and depravity. In addition, Asian immigration was likened to an invasion of the United States by foreigners who were incapable of assimilating into U.S. society—the same hollow arguments used by modern-day opponents of Mexican immigration.

And, as with the arbitrary numerical limitations that would one day be imposed on immigration from Mexico, the bans on Asian immigration of the late nineteenth and early twentieth centuries bore no relationship to economic and social reality and were therefore destined to fail from the

The Chinese Question

outset. The Chinese Exclusion Act of 1882 barred the entry of Chinese immigrants into the country, and the "Gentlemen's Agreement" between the United States and Japan of 1907 aimed for a similar prohibition against Japanese immigration. But the demand for Chinese and Japanese workers remained high, and the desire of these workers to bring their family members to the United States also remained high. The predictable result was twofold: Chinese and Japanese immigrants took advantage of loopholes in the exclusion laws to enter the country legally, and they took advantage of gaps in U.S. immigration enforcement to enter illegally.

It is impossible to say how many undocumented Asian immigrants made it into the United States during the period that they were barred from doing so legally. The federal government estimates that 17,300 Chinese immigrants crossed the Mexican and Canadian borders without papers between 1882 and 1920. But other sources indicate that twenty-seven thousand undocumented Chinese and Japanese immigrants entered the United States during just the decade from 1910 to 1920. At any rate, it is clear that undocumented Asian immigration occurred along both the northern and southern borders, and via the Pacific, Atlantic, and Gulf Coasts.

According to Lee, the first undocumented Asian immigrants were probably Chinese workers who came to the United States legally to work on the railroads, but who then went north to work on the Canadian Pacific Railway. They found themselves stuck in Canada when the Chinese Exclusion Act passed in 1882, which prohibited them from legally reentering the United States. Given how sparse defenses were along the four-thousand-mile U.S.-Canada border, paying to be smuggled into the United States was a reasonable option. In 1909, a reporter found that between two and four Chinese immigrants were smuggled into Buffalo each week at a cost of $200–$600 each. Cost notwithstanding, illicit border crossing was sometimes a fatal endeavor. The Bureau of Immigration reported in 1906 that a Chinese migrant froze to death during a snowstorm while hiding in a rail car full of ice, and six migrants drowned while trying to cross Lake Erie.

Crossing the U.S.-Canada border was the simplest way for a Chinese migrant to get into the United States until 1923, when Canada passed its own Chinese exclusion legislation. But even as early as the 1890s, Chinese migrants were also crossing the U.S.-Mexico border. This became an even more popular route with the introduction in 1902 of regular steamship travel between China and Mexico. While some who made the journey to Mexico ultimately settled there, the majority continued northward into the United States. El Paso in particular was known as a hotbed for smuggling Chinese immigrants in from Mexico. Similarly, the persistence of Japanese immigration via both Canada and Mexico even after the 1907 Gentlemen's Agreement led some observers to worry that U.S. borders were out of control—another common argument made by nativists today.

The entry of so many undocumented migrants would not have been possible without a formidable smuggling business. Steamship companies and labor agencies were either directly involved or turned a blind eye to what was obviously going on. A transnational network of guides, agents, smugglers, and corrupt immigration officials was instrumental in facilitating the movement of migrants across the border. There were even brokers who would—for the right price—arrange for steamship tickets, identity papers, witnesses, and attorneys. And migrants en route to the United States depended upon family and friends who were already there for money, maps, directions, and Chinese-English or Japanese-English dictionaries. Some of the people involved in people smuggling had experience in the smuggling of alcohol and opium. But others took advantage of their legitimate occupations in various border locales to cash in on the flow of Asian migrants. At times, Asian immigrants tried to cross the border in disguise; pretending to be Native American when crossing from Canada into the United States, and Mexican when crossing from Mexico.

In response to the growth of undocumented Asian immigration, the federal government began pouring more resources into both northern and southern border enforcement in the early nineteen hundreds. To start with, major investigations were launched to determine the scope of the problem. One such investigation, by an Immigrant Inspector named Marcus Braun, produced a multivolume report in 1907 that detailed not only the smuggling of Chinese and Japanese immigrants, but also

European and Middle Eastern immigrants seeking to avoid the prohibition against immigration by persons likely to become "public charges" (that is, dependent upon government assistance to survive). Stacked up against these often elaborate smuggling operations, U.S. efforts at border enforcement were inadequate, to say the least. In 1909, two years after Braun's report, there were a total of three hundred employees of the U.S. Bureau of Immigration arrayed along both the northern and southern borders. Given the thousands of miles of borderlands, three hundred people could cover very little ground.

Enforcement efforts evolved very differently along the northern and southern borders. To the north, U.S. officials relied heavily upon diplomacy; convincing Canadian authorities to allow U.S. immigration inspectors to enforce U.S. immigration laws in Canada on arriving steamships and at specially designated border points. Under U.S. pressure, Canada even adopted its own anti-Chinese immigration law in 1923. To the south, however, Mexico was not as cooperative—viewing Chinese immigration as an exclusively U.S. problem and refusing to let U.S. immigration officers operate on Mexican soil. And so the federal government adopted a more unilateral approach to southern border enforcement based on surveillance of the movements of Chinese immigrants in Mexico (using not only U.S. immigration officers, but a network of informants in both Mexico and the United States), creation of the first border patrols meant to deter undocumented entry into the United States, and immigration raids, arrests, and deportations targeting undocumented immigrants. Special agents known as "Chinese catchers" were specifically charged with finding and arresting undocumented Chinese immigrants.

In yet another harbinger of the future, all of these enforcement efforts succeeded primarily in redirecting undocumented migration through more remote (and dangerous) routes and increasing the demand for fraudulent identity documents. For instance, when U.S. border enforcement intensified in California and Arizona, smugglers turned increasingly to crossings in Texas and New Mexico. Even the Caribbean and Gulf of Mexico became people-smuggling routes, with undocumented Chinese migrants hiding in boats full of fruit making runs from Cuba to Florida. During the 1910s, Jamaica had become a way station for Chinese migrants. And migrants already in the United States traded identities and immigration papers with intending migrants who were still in China.

With each new immigration restriction enacted by the federal government, a whole new stream of undocumented immigration was created. When the 1921 Quota Act restricted immigration from southern and eastern Europe, undocumented immigrants from Europe and the Middle East appeared in increasing numbers at the northern and southern borders. By the 1920s, many U.S. officials had come to accept that U.S. borders might be a deterrent to undocumented immigration, but not a barrier. And in 1927, Secretary of Labor James Davis said that undocumented immigration wouldn't be stopped even if the army were deployed along the land borders, the navy along the maritime borders, and a nine-thousand-mile long wall erected. However, in 1924 the federal government took a step in that direction with the creation of the U.S. Border Patrol.

Ironically, escalating U.S. border enforcement left Mexico in particular in a quandary over what to do with Chinese immigrants stuck on the Mexican side. This predicament, added to the world economic depression of the 1930s and the U.S. expulsion of one million Mexicans back to their home country, led Mexico to adopt a much harsher, anti-Chinese stance. Some Chinese relocated within Mexico to states less in the grip of anti-Chinese hysteria, others went back to China, and still others—more than twenty thousand—were expelled into the United States to become the problem of the U.S. Border Patrol.

THE IMPROBABLE LIFE OF DOCTOR Q

While most accounts of undocumented immigration are tales of deprivation and suffering, this one is a success story—an exceptional success story. It hinges not only on the powerful intellect and drive of one particular undocumented immigrant, but also on a rare historical opportunity for undocumented immigrants in the United States to acquire the legal status that enabled them to climb a few rungs up the socioeconomic ladder. Or, in the case of Alfredo Quiñones-Hinojosa, quite a few rungs.

Alfredo's life began, inauspiciously enough, with his birth in the village of Palaco, in Mexico's Baja Peninsula, in 1968. As he would one day write in his often poignant autobiography, he was the oldest of five children and lost his baby sister to diarrhea, which had led to a deadly case of colitis by the time she made it to a hospital.[5] When Alfredo was seven, his family lived in a two-bedroom house across the canal from his father's gas station. At that point, they were part of an emerging lower middle class that could eat at restaurants now and then, as well as afford meat once a week. The work ethic in his family was strong, so he was working at the gas station after school from the age of five on. He sometimes picked cotton as well. But he was also a child—and a hyperactive one at that—who spent many a night stargazing and fantasizing about having super powers like the heroes in the comic books he read. He also had nightmares in which his superpowers proved insufficient to save his family from disaster.

One day, when he was nine, he saw his father crying alone behind the house. He had lost the gas station. This was in part the product of a worsening economic crisis throughout all of Mexico, and in part to the fact that, as his father discovered very belatedly, the underground gas

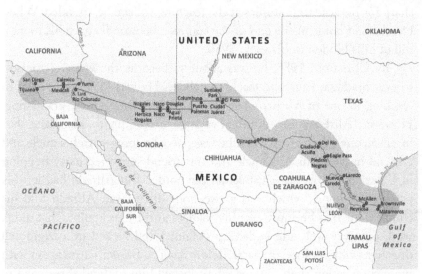

A Map of Mexico's Baja Peninsula Where Alfredo Quiñones-Hinojosa Was Born
IMAGE © ISTOCK.COM/RAINER LESNIEWSKI

tanks had been leaking into the earth for years. And so their lower middle class life evaporated, as did their standing in the community. For the first time they began to experience hunger. And his father turned increasingly to alcohol to cope. In the meantime, his mother stepped up and got creative. She opened a secondhand shop in a market outside of Palaco. She also bought an old sewing machine and, at night, made risqué outfits for prostitutes at the neighborhood brothel. But this was not sufficient to make ends meet; nor was the generosity of one of Alfredo's uncles, who lived and worked part time in the United States.

And so, in consultation with another uncle—who was a foreman at a big ranch in California—the family decided to head north one summer to work as crop pickers in Mendota. They didn't have work permits, but they did have passports that allowed them to cross the border as tourists. Alfredo was eleven at the time and although he didn't work in the fields, he did help out at the garage and clean workers' rooms. When he was fourteen he went back to Mendota in the summer to work in the fields by himself; first pulling weeds, then gradually working his way up to picking cotton and tomatoes, working the sorting and counting machines, and—finally—driving tractors. During his breaks he read to keep his mind sharp for his academic studies at the teaching college he attended. When he returned home at the end of the summer, he proudly gave his mom a roll of bills hidden in his sock: $950.

By Christmas 1985, he was about to become the youngest person to ever graduate from the teaching college. He was looking forward to teaching in one of Mexico's better elementary schools after graduating. However, Alfredo's life didn't always go according to his plans. For instance, one glitch arose when he was party hopping with his uncle and a friend in Mexicali. His uncle and this friend suggested party hopping in Calexico, California—just across the border. But Alfredo had left his passport at home, which was a two-hour drive away. Alfredo told his companions that he'd just take his chances at the checkpoint. That didn't work out very well. He ended up detained and locked in a frigid cell overnight with no food or water. Before dawn, a Border Patrol agent with more compassion than the one who'd locked him up (and threatened to hurt his family, too) let him go and gave him money for breakfast.

Another, far bigger glitch in Alfredo's plans materialized when he was assigned to a school in a remote rural area of Mexico. The better, city jobs had gone to kids from wealthier families with more political connections. He became depressed and disillusioned. But then he decided to adjust his plan a bit. He would attend a university without any outside help, saving up what he earned doing agricultural work. He'd also save enough to buy a used car (he eventually got an old Thunderbird).

At the end of 1986, Alfredo set out with a friend and a couple of cousins to work for a few weeks before Christmas and earn some holiday money. This time, he made sure to have his passport on him. But a suspicious Border Patrol agent pulled him and his friend aside for two hours of questioning about where they had gone in the United States during their previous trips and why. They dutifully responded that they visited family, but the agent wasn't buying it. Then he grabbed Alfredo's wallet, opened it, and saw all of the U.S. pay stubs that were inside. They'd been working without work permits. He and his friend had their passports confiscated and were told to go back to Mexico. For some unfathomable reason, this event firmly set Alfredo on a course he had contemplated before: going to the United States for a much longer period of time than he'd ever gone before to see if he could find there the opportunities that seemed to be eluding him in Mexico. He planned to do so on New Year's Day, 1987.

His first attempt—a run, climb, and jump over the border fence just a little outside of the Mexicali city limits—ended with immediate capture by a nice enough pair of Border Patrol agents who booked him, accepted the fake name he provided, then sent him back to Mexico. But then he tried nearly the same move again, and at the same place as before. This time, however, he studied the motions of the Border Patrol agents beforehand and timed his fence hopping a little better. And this time he made it without being caught. One of his uncles was waiting on the other side and drove him to the San Diego airport for phase 2 of the mission: avoiding land-based immigration checkpoints by taking a short flight to Los Angeles—hopefully without having to showing any ID. On the way to the airport, his uncle taught him how to say, in English, "A ticket to Los Angeles, please." A smuggler might have charged $600 for comparable service, but Alfredo only had sixty-five dollars, so he took his chances, struck gold with an airline agent who—in this pre-9/11 era—didn't ask for ID, and paid sixty-three dollars for his ticket. Then, on January 2—his nineteenth birthday—he and his uncle (who had met him in Los Angeles in Alfredo's Thunderbird) headed for the San Joaquin Valley.

Alfredo now learned the many joys of being a year-round migrant farmworker. First and foremost was the fact that he was constantly on the move from farm to farm and crop to crop as growing seasons changed. As a result, he was always starting over, at the bottom of the job ladder, despite his obvious mechanical and driving skills. He also had the experience of living in his car for a few weeks to save up the $300 needed to buy a leaky camping trailer that could serve as his home no matter what farm he was at. But he decided to view all the adversities he encountered as challenges—educational tests of his unstoppable drive. His sometimes absurd degree of overconfidence wavered at times, as when he found himself moving irrigation lines in the winter in muddy fields, his feet worn raw and bloody. He daydreamed about returning to his home one day a wealthy and successful man, but that dream seemed doubtful at times in the face of a $3.75 per hour paycheck. Still, he learned focus and patience from his agricultural work, and at each new farm was able to move up the job ladder quickly by demonstrating his skills, until he was head of a crew or the operator of some complex piece of farm machinery.

It wasn't quite as easy to overcome the dehumanizing way he was so frequently treated by the English-speaking owners of the farms. They kept interaction with the workers to a minimum and treated them as if they were faceless ciphers. He learned from this that he must never reduce the totality of a human being to their job. It was also apparent that the key to really getting ahead was more education—especially learning English. He was encouraged in this by a cousin who was excelling at Fresno State. Fortunately, recent changes in U.S. immigration law gave him a life-changing opportunity that comes along very rarely. The 1986 immigration reform legislation signed into law by a Republican president (Ronald Reagan) allowed qualified agricultural workers who were undocumented to apply for work authorization, which in turn would allow him to attend college. Moreover, he could eventually apply for a green card as well, and then U.S. citizenship. So Alfredo filed his paperwork for work authorization and waited for it to be approved.

Alfredo's family eventually joined him in the United States—including his parents, who went farther north to look for work in a more urban environment. They were disappointed that he seemed to be on the road to the life of an agricultural worker rather than a more intellectual pursuit. However, Alfredo's career in agriculture was abruptly cut short by a conversation with one of his cousins, who worked at a ranch where Alfredo also worked. When Alfredo mentioned that he was thinking of going to night school to become more proficient in English, his cousin laughed and told Alfredo that was a waste of time. According to his cousin, Alfredo was right where he belonged and would spend the rest of his life in the fields. But it was against Alfredo's nature to simply give in to this bleak vision of his future. He rebelled against it. He told his boss he was going on break and left the fields forever. In two days time he had joined his parents in Stockton, where they were staying with relatives.

The next phase of his life began with night classes at San Joaquin Delta Community College—and a job at the port shoveling sulfur and scraping the greasy remnants of fish from the bottom of ships. Just when he'd about had his fill of fish entrails (and the taunts of a couple of coworkers, including one who was Chicano, that he was a stupid, lazy wetback), a relative got him a job on a welding team for California Railcar Repair, which refurbished tanker cars. He started as a janitor in the shed, then—when he'd moved up to welding—was able to get his father to replace him as janitor. His welding career was a bit rocky, however. He once put his eye shield on wrong and burned his corneas. It was a mistake he made only once.

But lying unconscious at the bottom of a railway tanker car that had been used to haul petroleum proved to be an even bigger mistake. In 1989, after removing the lid of the tanker, he dropped one of the nuts down the hole. In an ill-advised attempt to retrieve the nut, he shimmied down a rope into the tanker, where he was quickly overwhelmed by the fumes and nearly went unconscious. He managed to climb the rope almost all the way to the top and clasp the hand of one of his coworkers, but the coworker couldn't hold on and Alfredo fell eighteen feet back down to the bottom of the tanker.

Alfredo's brother-in-law went in after him, and was unconscious by the time he made it to the bottom. He regained consciousness long enough to roll Alfredo onto his back, revealing his purple face and foaming mouth. But, before his brother-in-law could secure Alfredo with the rope he carried, he was driven out of the tanker by the fumes. He passed out as he was dragged from the tanker, but regained consciousness quickly and went in again, moving faster this time. He managed to get a rope around Alfredo before being driven out again by the fumes. This time Alfredo's coworkers were able to pull him out.

Alfredo was taken by pickup truck to an industrial clinic, where an ambulance then ferried him to the hospital. He was put in an oxygen tent, medical tests followed, and—despite being unable to form coherent sentences for a few hours—there were no signs of oxygen deprivation. Everyone, even the doctors, found this stroke of good luck to be inexplicable. In fact, Alfredo felt as though his brain had been permanently supercharged by this flirtation with death. He felt more focused, more positive in outlook. He watched his doctor at work; he listened to his father telling him that he'd been given a gift and should use it to help others; and he felt that he was on a new path in life.

Alfredo excelled in community college, although he did not realize until the third semester that an associate degree is not the same as a bachelor's degree and that his educational journey was just beginning. He ditched his welding job and got one at a mall that involved selling imported designer men's clothing. He also joined the debate club to improve his English and did track-and-field to burn off the extra energy he had acquired after his near-death accident in the tanker car. And, of course, he applied to universities. Two of his acceptances came from the University of California at Berkeley and Stanford University. He chose Berkeley, where he also excelled, although he still had to deal with racist jibes. For instance, even his teaching assistant in anthropology was ignorant enough to once comment to him, "You can't be from Mexico. You're too smart to be from Mexico."

After Berkeley, he went on to Harvard Medical School in 1994. He soon learned that many of his classmates came from very old, wealthy, and Anglo backgrounds that were very different from his own. Not surprisingly, it was only a matter of time before a fellow med student proclaimed that the only reason Alfredo "got into Harvard is because of quotas." Regardless, he eventually decided on becoming a surgeon, and—later—a brain surgeon. Naturally, by choosing such an illustrious career path, he ran repeatedly into racist preconceptions about what he could or should do in the field of medicine. "You really don't know what it takes to be a brain surgeon" (translation: "you come from an underdeveloped country, so you're out of your league"). "You should really become a primary care physician" (translation: "you're Mexican, and lots of poor Mexican communities in the United States need doctors").

Despite the strenuous demands and financial strains of medical school, Alfredo found time to build a complete life with firm roots in his adopted homeland: he married a woman he'd met years before in community college, he cultivated a wide and diverse range of friends, he became a U.S. citizen, he became a father, and he gave the commencement speech at the class graduation. It was also at Harvard that Alfredo was dubbed "Doctor Q" because so many people found his full last name to be unpronounceable.

After Harvard, Dr. Q went on to land a residency in neurosurgery at the University of California, San Francisco. It was there, right around Labor Day 1999, that he found himself assisting with the care of a patient with advanced AIDS (and Hepatitis C). The doctor in charge was using a large hollow-bore needle to drain fluid from the patient's body, and the needle slipped out and stabbed Dr. Q deep in the wrist. Dr. Q was informed that it would take one year before it was known definitively whether he had contracted HIV or not—although the odds were not in his favor. He'd have to take the triple-drug anti-AIDS cocktail for one month—along with the exhaustion, vomiting, and diarrhea it caused—just in case he did have HIV. As with his fall in the tanker car years before, Dr. Q again beat the odds. One year later he received an AIDS-free bill of health and promptly became the father to a second child—and then a third.

He eventually landed at Johns Hopkins University in Baltimore, Maryland, where he became Associate Professor of Neurosurgery and Oncology, as well as director of the Brain Tumor Surgery Program and head of the Brain Tumor Stem Cell Laboratory. Dr. Q's path from the fields to the operating room is inspirational, exceedingly rare, and illustrates the power inherent in one particular immigration policy: legalization of undocumented immigrants. Without that, Dr. Q's journey would not have been possible no matter how brilliant and highly motivated he was.

CHAPTER FIVE

Fearing the Unknown

AMERICAN ATTITUDES TOWARDS NEWCOMERS, LIKE THE AMERICAN sense of identity itself, have always been complex and contradictory. After all, the colonies that would one day become the United States were founded by refugees from religious persecution who, once they were settled, had to decide who among the new groups of people still arriving in North America were "outsiders" and who were "insiders." The early consensus seemed to be that God had meant Anglo-Saxons to be on top. The arrival of too many people from outsider groups threatened that God-given status. So, for instance, in the early seventeen hundreds, a sense of panic was instilled in the leaders of Pennsylvania—among them Benjamin Franklin—when so many Germans were arriving that it threatened to "Germanize" the entire colony. Indeed, by midcentury, nearly half the colony was of German extraction.[1]

The Founding Fathers were full of contradictions between their ideals and the way they treated others. In the Declaration of Independence, Thomas Jefferson indicted King George for obstructing the naturalization of foreigners. Yet, six years later in 1782, Jefferson was warning about the dangers of accepting immigrants who came from societies ruled by monarchs and who therefore didn't know anything about democracy. This was a far cry from the concept that "all men are created equal," as well as the radical philosophy behind the American Revolution—that one became an American by choice, not birth.

Put differently, nativism has always existed in the United States, even before it was the United States. What changes from generation to generation is who qualifies as a "native" and who is the "foreigner" or "alien" looking in from the outside. But while nativists are always present, they are not always in charge of immigration law and policy. In fact, as political scientist Daniel J. Tichenor points out, until the 1880s, North American nativists lacked the political power to exclude immigrants of any nationality. They tried for decades to keep out the Irish and the Germans, but to no avail. They formed their own political parties (the American Republican Party in the 1840s and the American Party of the 1850s), and they tried to influence both major political parties (the Whigs and the Republicans), yet achieved no enduring impact on the U.S. immigration system.

Nativists in the Federalist Party were briefly successful at changing immigration law in the 1790s, however. Riding a wave of anti-French sentiment, the Federalists—who controlled both houses of Congress and the presidency—passed the Alien and Sedition Acts of 1798. These laws extended the residency period for naturalization from five to fourteen years. They also granted the federal government the authority to deport foreigners who were citizens of a hostile nation—meaning France—or any non-citizen whom the president deemed to be a threat. The laws even restricted anti-government speech by U.S. citizens. But the Federalist grip on power was fleeting. The Democratic–Republican Party of Thomas Jefferson assumed power in 1801 and undid the Federalist immigration measures.

One reason for the initial failures of the nativists was that immigration was in the hands of the states—not the federal government. It wasn't until 1876 that immigration even became an exclusively federal issue, thanks to a Supreme Court ruling which found that state and local immigration laws infringe upon the power of Congress to regulate foreign commerce. Beyond the legalities of the issue is the fact that the United States had an acute need for more workers and more settlers. Both the Louisiana Purchase in 1803 and the treaty ending the Mexican-American War in 1848 opened up massive amounts of land for settlement. Plus, the spread of the Industrial Revolution to the United States in the middle of the century created a rapidly growing industrial economy that generated a lot of labor demand. So immigration—even the large-scale immigration that began in the latter part of the eighteen hundreds—was in the best interest of a broad swath of political and economic elites. Democrats in particular stood to gain from immigration since they had aligned themselves with the interests of immigrants from the very beginning. But even Whigs and Republicans with an anti-immigrant bent were intermittently pro-immigrant because they recognized the economic clout of immigrants, not to mention their voting power.

Nevertheless, the massive increase in immigration in the latter half of the nineteenth century did spark a powerful xenophobic response in many Americans. Catholics in particular—both Irish and German—were the target of much overheated political rhetoric about the evils of immigration. For instance, a common nativist belief was that Catholics could never be good U.S. citizens because their allegiance lay with the Vatican and the pope. Drawing upon that conspiracy theory, Samuel Morse, the inventor of the telegraph, warned in 1841 that the Vatican was dispatching Catholic immigrants to the United States in order to undermine democratic government and replace it with theocracy. As farfetched as that may sound today, these sorts of accusations sometimes went beyond wordplay in the nineteenth century and fueled anti-Catholic mob violence.

As the century wore on, the targets of nativist ire shifted. Although anti-Catholic bigotry certainly did not end after the Civil War, a growing share of nativist anger was redirected at immigrant groups that appeared even more dissimilar to a Protestant native than an Irish Catholic: Italians, Poles, Russians, Romanians, Turks, and Armenians. This anger was given scientific-sounding justification at the end of the century by the emerging field of eugenics, which favored the selective breeding of human beings in order to weed out supposedly inferior genetic traits. Not surprisingly, most of the allegedly superior traits just happened to be those possessed by people of northwestern European heritage.

But theories about racial inferiority meant to exclude certain groups weren't the only factor at play in determining who was in and who was out. After the Civil War, states not only had to make up for the population they had lost in the war itself, but they needed more workers to support rapid industrialization in the East and Midwest, the opening of the West through the construction of new railroads, and the land settlement made possible by the Homestead Act (which made millions of acres of federal land open to settlement by anyone who could put the land to productive use within five years). So much land was opened up that many states—including Kansas, Missouri, Nebraska, Iowa, and Colorado—began actively recruiting foreign workers by advertising abroad and negotiating low ship and train fares for would-be immigrants. Railroad companies also engaged in aggressive (and frequently false) advertising, as did steamship companies. An interesting pattern emerged in which the East and California were urbanizing and industrializing, while the rural interior was expanding. Both of these trends left nativists in a difficult position when they tried to argue that the latest wave of immigrants was socially and economically harmful.

Still, the nativists gave it their best shot. At the end of the century, for instance, three alumni of Harvard University formed the Immigration Restriction League. The League wanted a literacy test to be a requirement of immigration to the United States, which would have eliminated most of these new immigrants. One of the League's most stalwart supporters on Capitol Hill was Representative (and future senator) Henry Cabot Lodge (R-MA) who, in 1891, wrote of the new generation of immigrants as transients who were uninterested in the welfare of the United States and who never became U.S. citizens. He derided them as uneducated and unskilled laborers who reduced wages through ruinous job competition, carried disease, and were prone to criminality and violence. While he accused all immigrants from southern and eastern Europe of these transgressions, he reserved most of his vitriol for Italians. Lodge even spoke sympathetically of a nativist mob that lynched eleven Italians indicted for the assassination of New Orleans police chief David Hennessy in 1891.

Lodge argued that the United States no longer had the capacity to absorb and assimilate so many immigrants—particularly given the closing of the Western frontier at the end of the nineteenth century. Lodge believed that there was no more land to be settled, and that an oversupply of workers in industrial urban areas was putting downward pressure on wages—which he blamed on the immigrants themselves rather than the

Henry Cabot Lodge, 1850–1924

THE MIRIAM AND IRA D. WALLACH DIVISION OF ART, PRINTS AND PHOTOGRAPHS: PRINT
COLLECTION, THE NEW YORK PUBLIC LIBRARY. "HENRY CABOT LODGE, 1850–1924." NEW
YORK PUBLIC LIBRARY DIGITAL COLLECTIONS. ACCESSED DECEMBER 4, 2017. HTTP://
DIGITALCOLLECTIONS.NYPL.ORG/ITEMS/510D47E3-28D3-A3D9-E040-E00A18064A99

economic system in which they existed. This argument is repeated almost
verbatim by modern-day nativists, such as Mark Krikorian of the Center
for Immigration Studies, when discussing Mexican and Central American immigrants.[2] Ironically, Krikorian is the grandson of Armenian
immigrants, who were singled out as unfit by Lodge in 1891.[3]

While nativists weren't successful in curbing immigration from their least favorite European countries, they did ultimately succeed when it came to immigrants from China, who began to arrive in California in 1848 after the gold rush. The Chinese were initially welcomed by California's governor, but the welcome quickly wore off in the eyes of many white settlers who viewed them as exceedingly foreign—and therefore inferior.[4] Their language, style of dress, customs, favorite foods, skin color, and facial appearance were all suspect. It was commonly believed that the very presence of Chinese immigrants spread all manner of physical and moral ills to the white population, ranging from leprosy and prostitution to polygamy and paganism. Naturally, the delegates at the California constitutional convention of 1849 chose to grant the right to vote to white men only and not "inferior races." Organized labor was also heavily anti-Chinese. When the owners of mines and railroads exploited Chinese workers in order to suppress wages for everyone, the unions tended to blame the Chinese rather than the owners who were profiting from the exploitation.[5]

The Civil War dampened the furor of the anti-Chinese movement, but only temporarily. By the 1870s, as unemployment soared in California at the same time Chinese immigration reached record highs, anti-Chinese sentiment grew—and not only in California. The western delegations in Congress joined with anti-immigrant factions from the Northeast to push for immigration restrictions. In 1876, a Joint Special Committee to Investigate Chinese Immigration was formed to provide a pseudo-intellectual facade behind which lawmakers could hide their racism. The committee's majority report reached a number of dubious conclusions, such as the insufficient "brain capacity" of the Chinese to govern themselves.[6] It took until 1882, but the Chinese Exclusion Act eventually became a reality. Not only was future immigration from China prohibited, but Chinese immigrants already in the United States could not become U.S. citizens.

While nativist lawmakers were overjoyed at having succeeded in keeping Chinese immigrants out of the country, their work was by no means done. They still hadn't managed to achieve their original objective, which was to keep out the southern and eastern Europeans. And so they continued to make their case for further immigration restrictions and to form new alliances with like-minded interest groups. Their strength in Congress grew as well, bolstered by special commissions which released massive reports full of "scientific" evidence as to why Italians and Hungarians were genetically inferior to Germans and Swedes.

By the time World War I erupted in 1914, Social Darwinism had taken hold of the immigration debate with a vengeance and there was a veritable campaign in place to persuade good white women to produce more babies so that dark-skinned peoples wouldn't overrun the world. Even President Theodore Roosevelt spoke of the perils of "race suicide." In the first two decades of the twentieth century, there appeared a Eugenics Records Office, Race Betterment Foundation, and Human Betterment Foundation. Prominent scientists and intellectuals jumped on the eugenics bandwagon, including Alexander Graham Bell.

Studies were conducted that purported to show that, say, two out of every five immigrants were "feebleminded." One scientist advised that immigrant morons can be trained early to not become criminal or violent, but their employers must realize that they are like children in the ways they think and behave. However, by the 1930s many eugenicists were recanting their positions after their earlier work was shredded by numerous scientists (including Franz Boas, the father of American anthropology).

Dubious eugenic research was not the only factor driving debates about immigration during these decades. After World War I ended, there were major strikes and political demonstrations led by foreign-born communists and anarchists. Among ruling elites, this raised fears that Bolshevism was creeping into the U.S. working class from Russia following that country's revolution in 1917. Fear turned to alarm in 1919 when the home of Attorney General A. Mitchell Palmer was bombed, and around three dozen mail bombs were found addressed to all manner of political and corporate power brokers. All of this turmoil provoked what came to be known as the Palmer Raids—a crackdown on communists and anarchists, both native-born and immigrant. Hundreds of foreign radicals were deported, including one U.S. citizen (Emma Goldman, an anarchist who was born in Russia). These events morphed into the full-fledged panic and paranoia of the Red Scare. Communists were presumed to be lurking everywhere, and practically all immigrants were under suspicion.

In 1924, nativists who were fearful that genetically challenged immigrants would beat them in the job market and radicalize their children finally succeeded in imposing numerical quotas on immigration to the United States. The quotas varied by national origin: northern and western Europeans were in, and everybody else was effectively out—except for Mexicans and other inhabitants of the Western Hemisphere, who were left outside of the quota system due to their usefulness as easily exploited agricultural laborers. That same year, the first congressional appropriation for creation of the U.S. Border Patrol was made in order to stop the smuggling into the country of bootleg liquor and undocumented immigrants (mainly from China and Europe).

In 1929, unlawful entry into the United States was made a crime (a misdemeanor the first time; a felony the second). And in the early 1930s, during the Great Depression, President Herbert Hoover began a "repatriation" program; meaning mass deportations of Mexicans (and people of Mexican descent), in order the free up jobs for unemployed Americans. Hundreds of thousands of people were summarily dumped on the Mexican side of the border, regardless of their legal status, and left to fend for themselves.

It is sobering to keep in mind just how strong the headwinds of racism and nativism were at this time. The Ku Klux Klan reached its peak in the mid-1920s, with between two and five million members. A wide range of preachers, activists, and political movements fomented xenophobia and anti-Semitism, which fostered discrimination at every level of society, influencing who got to attend what university, work for what company, or live in what neighborhood. Even the revered industrialist Henry Ford was an anti-Semite and much admired by Adolf Hitler, who awarded him a swastika-adorned medal in 1938.

Other than its roots in white supremacy, another key feature of the immigration system after 1924 was that it ran on two tracks. The first, controlled by the State Department and its overseas consulates, enforced the quotas which kept out Asians and most Europeans. The second, run by the Labor Department and its Immigration Bureau, brought large numbers of Mexican guest workers into the United States (in 1942 this was formalized into the Bracero program, which lasted until 1964). As a result, European Jews seeking refuge from the rising tide of fascism were out of luck. But a grower in California seeking temporary hands at harvest time had no trouble importing Mexican workers. Although nativists generally opposed admitting Mexicans outside of the quota system (even on a temporary basis), they were unable to overcome the political clout wielded by the nation's growers, who argued that they needed Mexicans to perform jobs deemed unworthy of a white man. It is telling that the Bracero program was still in full swing when the mass deportation known as Operation Wetback was launched in 1954, revealing the extent to which the U.S. government regarded Mexicans as disposable workers.

After 1924, admitting anyone except temporary workers from Mexico was a struggle, usually between a Congress dominated by nativists and presidents who found that the national origins quota system hampered their foreign policy goals. At the end of World War II, for instance, nativists didn't even want to let in refugees who had survived the Nazis or were escaping from communist countries. In the end, after much politicking by the White House, the nativist gatekeepers in Congress allowed four hundred thousand refugees to enter the country under the Displaced Persons Acts in 1948 and 1950 (plus forty thousand allowed in by a presidential directive in 1945). This act of humanity stands in stark contrast to the federal government's imprisonment of one hundred ten thousand Japanese Americans on the West Coast at the beginning of the war.

Although the nativists were successful in preserving the quota system for decades (with some cosmetic modifications in 1952), their position was gradually eroding for a number of reasons. For one thing, the eugenic fantasies that formed the foundation of the quota system had been thoroughly discredited in scientific circles by the 1950s. In addition, at the height of the Cold War, it seemed hypocritical of the U.S. government to decry communism, but to not offer refuge to people who had fled communist regimes. Add to that the fact that the civil rights movement was growing; exposing the raw racism of a society that made African Americans second-class citizens, and made race the litmus test of its immigration system. And, finally, over the course of the four decades during which the quota system was in force, generations of immigrants had successfully integrated into U.S. society and given birth to very Americanized children. Even the Italians, derided by nativists for being incapable of assimilation, had obviously assimilated to the point of becoming "white" in the eyes of the larger society.

All of these forces reached a boiling point in 1965—one year after the Civil Rights Act became a reality. In the case of immigration, it was the Hart-Cellar Act that dismantled the national origins quota system. In its place was a more expansive system that allotted one hundred seventy thousand visas to immigrants from the Eastern Hemisphere (with a twenty thousand per-country limit) and one hundred twenty thousand for the Western Hemisphere (with no per-country limit, although one was added years later). Within these broad numerical caps, visas would go to the family members of legal immigrants (family members of U.S. citizens were—and still are—exempt from the caps), workers needed by U.S. employers, and refugees. The authors of the bill didn't expect it to have much of an effect on immigration overall, arguing that the benefits of the new system would flow primarily to Europeans with family members in the United States—not to Asians or Africans. In hindsight, the authors of the bill were obviously very wrong.

U.S. immigration patterns actually swung in exactly the opposite direction. For one thing, presidents had "parole" authority to go over the refugee limit (which they did repeatedly in the case of refugees from communist countries around the world). There was also growing economic inequality between the developed and less-developed world, which made the developed world an increasingly attractive destination for people who wanted a shot at a better life. And there were the myriad forces of globalization, which rendered the nations of the world increasingly interconnected in terms of trade, transportation, and communication. The end result was that over the course of the decades which followed the 1965 immigration law, millions of people from Latin America, the Caribbean, and Asia journeyed to the United States—some legally, some not.

Undocumented immigration from Latin America (especially Mexico) was the predictable result of a decision made in 1976 to add a twenty thousand visa per-country limit to the countries of the Western Hemisphere. What this meant was that massive Mexico, with its deep and long-standing ties to the United States, was placed under the same visa cap as tiny and isolated Paraguay. That made no sense given the deep dependence of U.S. employers—especially growers—on Mexican workers, and the large number of families that lived on both sides of the U.S.-Mexico border.

As immigration in general, and undocumented immigration in particular, increased throughout the 1970s and 1980s, the battle lines were drawn around the answer to a very basic question: was immigration a net benefit to the United States or was it a threat? On one side were organizations devoted to the advancement of rights for immigrants, refugees, Latinos, and Asians, which argued that immigrants were an economic and cultural asset to the nation. On the other side was a new breed of immigration restrictionist who argued that immigrants were a drain on our economy and a threat to our culture. Eschewing open racism, they argued instead that the United States was becoming overpopulated, that immigrants were draining our economic and natural resources, and that immigrants competed for scarce jobs, public services, housing, schools, etc. While these new nativists didn't use the terminology of eugenics and "racial betterment," the imagery provoked by their rhetoric was clear: the dark-skinned hordes of the developing world would overrun the light-skinned peoples of the developed world unless drastic action was taken. And, like their predecessors, modern nativists inaccurately stereotype immigrants as being prone to criminality and resistant to assimilation.

In the face of large-scale undocumented immigration—and in an attempt to balance the demands of employers, immigrant rights groups, and nativists—Congress tried in 1986 to fix the problem. Their formula, the Immigration Reform and Control Act (IRCA), called for the granting of legal status to most undocumented immigrants living in the country, increasing border enforcement, and offering "replenishment" of agricultural workers should legalization cause farm workers to leave the fields for other opportunities.

The law fell short for a couple of reasons. First of all, IRCA didn't create flexible avenues for future immigration to the United States. So, as the economic integration of the Western Hemisphere increased—a process which culminated in the North American Free Trade Agreement (NAFTA) of 1994—the movement of workers was not liberalized in the same way as the movement of commodities. Ironically, NAFTA's supporters had predicted that it would decrease undocumented migration by creating more jobs in Mexico. That didn't happen as planned. Competition from U.S. multinational corporations drove many Mexican workers out of their jobs or off of their farmland. And newly unemployed Mexicans knew that the best place to go in search of a new job was the United States.

A second reason for IRCA's long-term failure to stem undocumented immigration was the poor design and implementation of sanctions for employers who knowingly hired undocumented workers. Proving whether someone knowingly or unknowingly hires an undocumented immigrant is not an easy task. In part, this is because many of the numerous documents deemed acceptable as proof of legal residence in the United States were easily forged, and a whole document-forging industry arose after IRCA. Many employers could not tell whether or not a document was legitimate and, due to anti-discrimination laws also part of IRCA, had limited ability to question an employee about their documents. Even if an employer was clearly violating the law, criminal penalties were seldom imposed. Furthermore, labor laws were rarely enforced, which might have diminished the exploitation of workers in general, regardless of where they were born.

Another key development that changed the nature of immigration to the United States was the Refugee Act of 1980, which not only increased the number of refugees who could be brought into the country each year, but gave the president the power to exceed those limits in emergency situations. As a result, a growing number of refugees from around the world, from Cuba to Vietnam, were able to come to the United States. Sadly, though not surprisingly, refugee policy was warped by Cold War considerations. Refugees from Central America who were fleeing U.S.-backed authoritarian governments were typically denied refuge if they made it over the U.S.-Mexico border, while others, fleeing leftist regimes, were typically granted refuge.

In the post-NAFTA, post-IRCA era, hundreds of thousands of immigrants and refugees from every corner of the globe came to the United States each year for a new beginning. In the process, they created new neighborhoods or breathed life into old, decaying ones. But, as a result, the cultural landscape of many regions in the United States shifted dramatically.

Predictably, this transformation of U.S. society has provoked a nativist backlash. Some native-born Americans were irate that their tax dollars might pay for the education of children with undocumented parents. Others were incensed that they had to "press one for English, two for Spanish" when they called their bank. It was this anger that led to the passage of Proposition 187 in California in 1994, which would have denied virtually every public service (including education) to undocumented immigrants and their children—and would have required every public employee, from teachers to doctors, to report undocumented immigrants to federal authorities. Proposition 187 was authored by a paid advisor to an anti-immigrant organization, the Federation for American Immigration Reform (known implausibly as FAIR), a group which has taken money from the openly racist Pioneer Fund, the original mandate of which was to promote "human race betterment."

In the end, Proposition 187 was struck down as unconstitutional in federal court and never took effect. However, it did propel Republican Pete Wilson into the governor's mansion in 1994, thanks to his support for the initiative and a campaign based on nativist fears of an undocumented Mexican invasion of the state. Much to the chagrin of nativists, Wilson and Proposition 187 motivated tens of thousands of immigrants who were eligible to naturalize to actually do so and then register to vote—as Democrats. After that, most Republican candidates for statewide office in California were doomed, with the notable exception of Republican governor Arnold Schwarzenegger, who was relatively moderate on immigration issues.

During the early 1990s, in the midst of an economic recession, the federal government began fortifying the U.S.-Mexico border against undocumented immigration. There were more Border Patrol agents, new high-tech gadgets to detect unauthorized crossings, and hundreds of miles of fencing. Yet the end result wasn't fewer undocumented immigrants in the United States, but more. True, more died while crossing the border in remote locations in an attempt to evade the Border Patrol.

Border Fence Separating Mexico and the United States
IMAGE © ISTOCK.COM/REX_WHOLSTER

But, once they got here, they were more likely to stay. Whereas in the past they might have worked here for a few years and then gone home, perhaps later to return for a few more years of work, now they stayed permanently because crossing the border was so difficult. And they had their relatives join them in the United States rather than be forever separated from them.[7] As a result, the undocumented population grew from 3.5 million in 1990 to a high of 12.2 million in 2007.[8] Moreover, undocumented immigrants started to settle in southern and midwestern states not accustomed to a significant immigrant presence, provoking fear and hate in many native-born whites.

And it was fear and hate that went into three bills authored by nativist Republicans in Congress in 1996: the Illegal Immigration Reform and Immigrant Responsibility Act (IIRIRA), the Antiterrorism and Effective Death Penalty Act (AEDPA), and the Personal Responsibility and Work Opportunity Reconciliation Act (PRWORA). These bills made sweeping changes to immigration law, making it easier to deport or deny federal welfare benefits even to lawfully present immigrants. Much of the vitriol that went into the crafting of these provisions came from FAIR and one of its spin-offs, the Center for Immigration Studies (CIS), as well as from a leading immigration restrictionist in Congress, Lamar Smith from Texas. In the end, the goal of the immigration provisions of these laws was to make life as difficult as possible not only for undocumented immigrants, but for green-card holders as well. As with Proposition 187, the 1996 laws forcefully persuaded large numbers of eligible immigrants to acquire U.S. citizenship and become Democratic voters.

There have been a couple of failed efforts since 1996 to enact immigration reform that actually makes sense; giving undocumented immigrants already in the country the chance to acquire legal status, while making channels of legal immigration more flexible and responsive to changing economic conditions. One such attempt came in 2001, when an immigration accord with Mexico seemed possible. Unfortunately, the terrorist attacks of 9/11 put a quick end to that.

Instead, the government swiftly switched gears from immigration reform to religious profiling. A "special registration" program was implemented that required male noncitizens from twenty-four primarily Muslim countries to register with the government and be photographed and fingerprinted.

Congress tried twice more, in 2006 and 2007, to pass a reform bill. Each time, the bills were ultimately derailed by restrictionist Republicans, supported by a web of nativist thinkers, anti-immigrant organizations, and right-wing media personalities. Economist George Borjas and political scientist Samuel Huntington provided intellectual arguments for restriction; the network of anti-immigrant groups created by John Tanton—particularly FAIR and CIS—organized their members to weigh in; and radio and TV personalities such as Rush Limbaugh, Lou Dobbs, Sean Hannity, Bill O'Reilly, and Ann Coulter whipped up nativist sentiment in their viewers and listeners. The Republican majority in Congress embraced these nativists wholeheartedly, hiding behind the fig leaf of national security to justify themselves, and spent the rest of the decade thinking of new ways to make life miserable for the foreign-born. After its efforts to support immigration reform failed, the Bush administration began ramping up immigration raids on worksites in search of undocumented immigrants.

As the federal government dawdled on immigration reform, state and local governments stepped in to fill the void. Some voted to prevent police from inquiring about someone's immigration status, so that undocumented immigrants would feel free to report crimes. Others joined the 287(g) program, in which immigration enforcement agents train local police officers to act as immigration agents. Oakland, California, required all municipal departments to have bilingual employees on staff. Prince William County, Virginia, denied all county services of any kind to undocumented immigrants. And Hazleton, Pennsylvania, passed an ordinance making it a crime to rent an apartment to an undocumented immigrant. The end result was a complete mess; a patchwork of conflicting rules and regulations on topics that should have been decided at the federal level. In the first six months of 2008, for example, 1,267 new immigration bills were introduced in forty-five state legislatures, of which 175 laws and resolutions were passed in thrity-nine states. These bills were all over the map politically, and some were nonsensical (such as the bill in Pahrump, Nevada, making it illegal to fly the flag of a foreign country unless the U.S. flag is flying next to it).

One particularly high-profile battle at the state level concerns whether or not undocumented immigrants who are residents of a state are eligible for in-state college tuition or must pay the higher out-of-state (or out-of-country) rate. One aspect of this debate which makes it unique is that it applies mostly to undocumented immigrants who were brought to the United States as children and therefore were never given the choice as to whether or not they wanted to come here. A number of states, including California and Texas, allowed eligible undocumented immigrants to pay in-state tuition rates. Many did not. South Carolina headed in the opposite direction and prohibited undocumented immigrants from attending state colleges and universities under any circumstances.

While some hot-button immigration issues change over time—like modern-day debates over 287(g) agreements and in-state tuition rates—what is even more remarkable is how little nativism changes. Whether the focus is on nineteenth century immigrants from Italy or twentieth century immigrants from Mexico, the fears of nativists remain the same: foreigners are stealing jobs from the native-born, they're not becoming "American" fast enough, they don't learn English fast enough. It's always a war between "us" and "them," but who "they" are changes every few decades.

THE ITALIAN MENACE

Italians have been a part of U.S. history from the beginning, albeit in small numbers at first.[9] Christopher Columbus was Italian, as were a number of other, early explorers/conquerors of North America, such as Giovanni Verrazzano and Giovanni Caboto (John Cabot). Nevertheless, even by the time of the Civil War, only ten thousand Italians were recorded as residents of the country. There were discernible Italian American communities in New York, Boston, and a few other cities, and Italian-language newspapers meant primarily for immigrants. But Italians were too few in number to serve as convenient targets for American nativists. There is little doubt that the anti-Catholic Know-Nothings in the 1850s disliked Italians and their Catholicism, but the far more numerous Irish and German Catholics were the focus of Know-Nothing ire.

All of this changed as the number of Italian immigrants started to rise in the latter half of the century. At first, these immigrants hailed from northern Italy and tended to be better-educated political exiles, craftsmen, and small entrepreneurs. Then came a trickle of generally poorer, less-educated immigrants from southern Italy. Since their numbers were relatively small, they evoked little nativist reaction. Still, newspapers of the time wrote of U.S. superiority to crime-ridden Italy, and Anglo-Saxon superiority to allegedly crime-prone Italian immigrants. This stereotype of the Italians (especially southern Italians) as born criminals would persist for well over a century. Italians were also portrayed in the newspapers and books of the time as ignorant, lazy, and prone to criminal activity.

Historian Salvatore LaGumina compiled many of these print accounts describing the Italian menace. On April 16, 1876, for instance, the *New York Times* pronounced that Italians have "a natural inclination toward criminality," which was said to be linked to laziness, deceitfulness, corruption, and a tendency to gossip. All of this applied doubly so to immigrants from southern Italy, where crime rings were said to rule the

Group of Italian Street Laborers, Working under Sixth Ave. Elevated, New York City, 1910

land. The *New York Times* also opined on November 12, 1875, about the stark difference between northern and southern Italians. The northerners were "industrious and honest," while the southerners were "extremely ignorant," "miserably poor," and "frequently guilty of crimes of violence"— so much so that it was probably "hopeless to think of civilizing them."[10]

Some Americans viewed Italian immigration as a "slave trade." This came in variations. A July 7, 1872, *New York Times* story spoke of children being purchased from their parents by criminals in Italy and used in the United States as beggars who play musical instruments very badly. A December 16, 1872, *New York Herald* story proclaimed that "ignorant peasants" in Italy were being duped into coming to the United States, where they become vagrants and beggars, making them victims of "the worst kind of white slave trade."

As offensive as all of this commentary is, it came during a period of relatively low immigration from Italy. During the 1880s, when Italian immigration turned from a trickle to a wave, nativist fear and loathing skyrocketed, even more so because this new immigrant flow was originating in southern Italy rather than the somewhat-more-acceptable north. The stereotypes that were lobbed at these immigrants were the same as those from the 1870s, but the context had changed. Before, Italians were an oddity. Now, arriving by the thousands, a growing number of Americans viewed them as a threat. Of course, all of the immigrants from southern and eastern Europe who started arriving en masse during the 1880s were also perceived as a threat by American nativists.

Many southern Italians made easy targets. They were illiterate in their own language, dressed in ragged yet colorful clothes, and were frequently seen begging in the street. As such, it took only a short leap of logic to ascribe horrible character flaws to them. For instance, the March 5, 1882, edition of the *New York Times* proclaimed that New York had never witnessed a group of immigrants "so low and ignorant" as the Italians. However, the story said that they were generally honest people who didn't commit robbery or theft. Instead, they appeared in court "continually" on charges of fighting and attempted murder among themselves, owing to the crowded and destitute conditions in which they lived. The big problem was the children of these immigrants, who were said to be of the "lowest and most degraded character" and were portrayed as not much better than a pack of wild dogs. Apparently, the children could only be saved by the Americanizing influence of schools run by charitable organizations. Otherwise, they would inevitably grow up to be criminals.

Italians in general were portrayed as born bandits or robbers. As a January 1, 1884, *New York Times* story put it, Italians come to the United States "with a hereditary respect" for banditry given the lowly conditions in which they were raised. In fact, so the story went, Italians actually respect banditry as a "noble career," which is not surprising considering that it is a "national industry." These bandits routinely kidnap people and hold them hostage for ransom, perhaps sending the ear or nose or finger of one of their victims to family members in order to persuade them to pay up.

Nativists of the nineteenth century, just like nativists today, were fond of outrageous immigrant-centered conspiracy theories. One of the more bizarre ones, described in a November 8, 1883, *New York Times* story, concerned an Italian plot to export fleas to the United States. The story begins with the discovery of an Italian flea in Pennsylvania, which is—naturally—"twice as malignant" as an American flea. Given that the Italian flea is found in communities of Italian immigrants, it stands to reason (apparently) that there was a deeply sinister plan afoot to flood the United States with Italian fleas that would make everyone so miserable that they'd vote for free trade, anti-protectionist legislation. In the nativist writer's estimation, what was needed was an exclusionary system like the Chinese Exclusion Act that keeps out "the pauper fleas of Europe." This sounds like satire, but it was not—which illustrates just how far down the rabbit hole a nativist can fall.

Anti-Italian sentiment hit a new high (or, rather, sank to a new low) between 1890 and 1914, when previous immigration records were shattered and more than 2.5 million Italians entered the country. This historic wave of immigration provoked hatred across a broad swath of organized labor due to fears that Italian workers would undercut the wages and take the jobs of native-born workers. In addition, Social Darwinism was on the rise and those Anglo men and women who subscribed to its racist tenets believed themselves to be genetically superior to Italians and all of the other southern and eastern Europeans who were coming to the United States. This helped to propagate all sorts of stereotypes about Italians as perpetually poor fools as well as criminals.

This era of Italian immigrant history began with a mass murder carried out by a lynch mob. In 1890, the police chief of New Orleans was killed by several men rumored to be Italian "Mafiosi." A police roundup of local Italian men quickly ensued and nineteen were held. Nine of these men were put on trial, but none were found guilty. Instead, six were acquitted and mistrials were declared in the other three cases. A lynch mob was promptly organized by several prominent native-born residents of New Orleans who believed that an egregious miscarriage of justice had occurred. The day after the trial, thousands of people gathered outside the city jail, broke inside, and murdered eleven of the nineteen Italians held there. No one was ever punished for the murders. Although other lynchings of Italians took place during this period, the New Orleans lynching was by far the worst.

A great many native-born commentators of the time defended the mob's actions on the assumption that the murdered men simply had to be Mafiosi because they were Italian. For instance, then-Representative Henry Cabot Lodge, a Republican from Massachusetts, wrote that while any "intelligent man deplores the lawless act of the New Orleans mob," it did "not spring from nothing without reason or provocation." Rather, the killings were "revenge"—a form of "wild justice." Lodge then uses the killings as an excuse to repeat every known stereotype about Italians. He deplores "the large number of Italians who stay but a short time in the United States, and who then return to their native country with such money as they have been able to save here." Lodge declares that this "is a most unwholesome feature in any immigration. Persons who come to the United States, reduce the rate of wages by ruinous competition, and then take their savings out of the country, are not desirable. They are mere birds of passage." He goes on to describe these itinerant Italians by stating that "they have no interest or stake in the country, and they never become American citizens." As he nears the end of his tirade, he throws in other southern and eastern Europeans for good measure, saying that "the increase of paupers is more alarming than that of criminals and diseased persons. Most of the Italians, Poles, and Hungarians have no money at all. They land in this country without a cent in their pockets."[11] These quotes are fascinating because they amount to the same hollow arguments used against Mexican and Central American immigrants by nativists today.

An example of just how fair and balanced press coverage was of the lynchings is provided by the October 17, 1890, *New Orleans Times-Democrat*, which saw fit to emphasize that the "jail was crowded with Sicilians, whose low, repulsive countenances, and slavery attire, proclaimed their brutal natures." This particular story ended with the assertions that the Italians remain isolated from everybody else in their communities, seldom learn English, and have no respect for U.S. laws or the U.S. system of government. They "are always foreigners."

It is also important to point out just how toxic the anti-Italian atmosphere was in New Orleans just prior to the lynchings. For instance, a newspaper called *The Mascot* published drawings that advocated killing Italians. One series of drawings suggested that they be drowned in batches. And another showed a cage full of Italian immigrants being lowered into the river, with the caption: "The Way to Dispose of Them." These were not subtle messages. They constituted an incitement to violence.[12]

THE LATINO THREAT

The nativist perspective on immigration from Latin America—Mexico, in particular—is illustrated well by the musings of political scientist Samuel P. Huntington.[13] In Huntington's opinion, Latin American immigrants are different from earlier waves of European immigrants in that they are not assimilating into U.S. society. Rather, they are forming "political and linguistic enclaves" in cities such as Los Angeles and Miami. In the process, they are "rejecting the Anglo-Protestant values that built the American Dream." Huntington thought that immigration from Mexico and elsewhere in Latin America was "the single most immediate and most serious challenge to America's traditional identity."[14] One can imagine nearly identical statements being made a century or so ago about Italians.

According to anthropologist Leo R. Chavez, a key component of this "Latino threat narrative" is the notion of "illegality." Immigrants from Mexico or Central America who come to or remain in the United States without authorization are commonly thought of as deserving no sympathy, no public services, no help. In reality, though, most immigrants—regardless of their legal status—are drawn to the United States by economic forces such as the demand for workers created by an aging population that is having fewer babies. What marks one immigrant as legal and another as illegal is whether or not U.S. society chooses to recognize the legitimacy of those economic forces. It amounts to a morbid political game in which lawmakers bow to nativist pressure by creating limits on immigration they know won't meet labor demands, and then call everyone who arrives in excess of those limits "illegal"—even though the economic roles played by immigrants who did not (or could not) come through legal channels are just as important as the roles played by the ones who did.

Mexicans became the stereotypical "illegal immigrants" in the 1920s, when new immigration laws not only created discriminatory quotas based on national origin, but also created the Border Patrol and required immigrants from Mexico and other points south of the border to submit to an inspection process. No numerical limits yet existed on immigration from Latin America. But those Latin American immigrants who bypassed U.S. border controls for some reason became "illegal aliens." And since the overwhelming majority of immigrants crossing the U.S.-Mexico border were Mexicans, they became inextricably linked to the concept of "illegality."

This was a relatively easy logical leap for many Americans to make. Given the continued popularity of eugenics in the 1920s, Mexicans were commonly viewed as an inferior "race" (along with the Chinese, who'd been barred from immigration and naturalization for decades). So it was no surprise that Mexicans were subject to segregation in the Southwest of the country much as African Americans were segregated in the Southeast. Even native-born children whose parents were from Mexico were viewed as perpetually "foreign" regardless of their U.S. citizenship. And while legalization programs for undocumented immigrants in the early twentieth century were open to Europeans, Mexicans were excluded. The act of crossing the border without permission was seen as inherently "criminal," and therefore a disqualification for legalization.

Beginning in the 1970s, and continuing up to the present, nativists took the idea of Mexican immigrants as criminals and kicked it up a notch. Mexican immigrants, especially of the undocumented variety, were portrayed not only as criminals, but as foreign invaders staging a long-term "reconquest" of the southwestern states that once belonged to Mexico. Allegedly, Mexican immigrants—as well as their children and grandchildren—maintain such a strong cultural attachment to their homeland that there is no room in their hearts or minds for an attachment to the United States as well. Of course, this is complete fantasy. There is abundant evidence that over time, and from generation to generation, immigrants—Mexicans included—learn English, adopt American customs, and integrate into U.S. society. Nevertheless, nativists continue to see a nefarious purpose in the existence of bilingual education programs that dare to teach Spanish as well as English (as if a human being is incapable of learning two languages at the same time), Chicano studies programs (learning about all aspects of one's heritage is apparently dangerous), and a student organization that's name contains a reference to the mythical Aztec homeland, "Aztlán" (clearly proof of secessionist intent).

The invasion myth involves more than just the fear of rampant immigration and radicalized U.S.-born Chicanos. It also encompasses the fear of rampant reproduction among Chicanas. This fear is tied up with the stereotype of Chicanas as "hot" women who love to have sex and therefore give birth to lots of children, which is thought by nativists to pose a demographic threat to Anglos as the Chicanos outbreed the Anglos until the Anglos one day are no longer the majority of the population. This doomsday scenario—which is contradicted by actual evidence on fertility rates among women in Mexico and Mexican women in the United States—motivated anti-immigrant zealots such as John Tanton (founder of the nativist Federation for American Immigration Reform, or FAIR) to sound the alarm about what eventually became known as the "browning" of America; or the supposed dilution of the white-skinned Anglo population by the rapidly reproducing darker-skinned Latino population.

This distorted and highly racialized view of the world is as much a fantasy as the racial hierarchies constructed by eugenicists a century before. Humans do not come in different breeds like dogs. The definition of any "race" is very slippery and has far more to do with culture than it does with biology. Melanin is not the enemy.

From multiple cover stories in *U.S. News and World Report* to a pair of books by Pat Buchanan, the image of an immigrant "invasion" is a potent symbol. In nativist mythology, Mexican women are assumed to give birth to children once they are in the United States only to gain a legal foothold here that will get them eventual U.S. citizenship (in a couple of decades); which is the idea behind the demeaning notion of the "anchor baby." The fact that even mainstream publications and intellectuals take seriously the idea that this separatist conspiracy has been in the works for centuries is evidence of just how powerful nativist mythology can be. Of course, this was not the only narrative being spun. In the latter half of the 1990s in particular, there were some conservative commentators who found themselves in agreement with some liberal labor unions that Mexican workers—including the undocumented—were adding value to a booming economy in need of labor.

And then came 9/11. Undocumented immigration, and the nature of the U.S.-Mexico border itself, took on a whole new meaning after that day. It was no longer just Mexican workers who might be sneaking across the border undetected; it was foreign terrorists. The fact that none of the 9/11 terrorists crossed the southern border or had any connection to Mexico was irrelevant. What mattered was that it *could* happen. And so sealing the border against unauthorized entry became a matter of national security, justifying billions of dollars in congressional appropriations for more Border Patrol agents, more border fencing, and more high-tech gadgetry to detect people trying to cross the border without permission. The invasion theme is still an integral part of the nativist mindset; but now it has a layer of homeland security on top.

This never-ending stream of rhetoric about Mexican invasions and Islamic terrorists sneaking through the Sonoran Desert to cross the border has not only persuaded many lawmakers to vote for more and more border-enforcement funding. It has also inspired quite a few civilians to don camouflage clothing, grab their assault rifles, and head to the U.S.-Mexico border to watch for anyone trying to cross. These self-styled defenders of the homeland first burst onto the national scene in 2005 in the form of the Minuteman Project, organized along the Arizona-Mexico border on April 1, intent upon doing their part to "seal the border" and keep undocumented immigrants, drug dealers, and terrorists out of the United States. While the Minutemen weren't very adept at catching "bad guys," they were rather savvy at commanding media attention and using it to disseminate their image of the U.S.-Mexico border as a war zone in dire need of patriotic defenders to pick up the slack left by a federal government which had abdicated its responsibility for national defense.

The Minuteman Project—founded in late 2004 by a California nativist named Jim Gilchrist—dressed itself up in patriotic symbols of all kinds: the American flag, the bald eagle, Uncle Sam, the Revolutionary War "Minuteman," and slogans like "Defending our borders." Another prominent slogan, "Americans doing the job government won't do," ignored the fact that the government had been pouring billions into border enforcement since 1986. Gilchrist chose to launch the Minuteman Project in Arizona—Cochise Country, in particular—because that is where a disproportionate share of undocumented border crossers were entering the country (having been diverted away from older crossing points in California and Texas by the concentrated deployment of new, federal border-enforcement resources). And Gilchrist chose a town—Tombstone—rich with wild west, cowboy symbolism.

From the very beginning, Gilchrist acknowledged that the Minutemen were more of a public-relations spectacle than a border-defense force. In fact, he claimed victory even before the first of his volunteers showed up in Arizona. That's because all the press surrounding the very existence of the project seemed to spur the federal government into deploying more Border Patrol agents along the Arizona-Mexico border and sending Homeland Security officials as well to draw attention to the federal government's efforts. (The government claimed the timing of its activities was purely coincidental.) When the two hundred or so Minuteman volunteers finally showed up at the beginning of April, the pageantry continued, with the Minutemen clad in camouflage clothing, strapping on bulletproof vests, and equipping themselves with walkie-talkies and guns. They fanned out in four-man teams along a twenty-three-mile stretch of border. They didn't actually catch any undocumented immigrants, but they did catch the interest of an extraordinary number of journalists—and, in so doing, put an international spotlight on the issue of undocumented immigration.

The Minuteman Project ceased operation after only three weeks, but it continued to make its presence felt. Border "monitoring" continued—for a while—under the watchful eye of Chris Simcox—a former teacher in Los Angeles turned anti-immigrant agitator in Arizona—and his Civil Homeland Defense organization. Gilchrist himself kept the issue alive in his unsuccessful run for Congress in Orange County, California, in 2005. And the Minuteman Project inspired quite a few imitations in Texas, New Mexico, California, Idaho, and Michigan. But the Minuteman experiment did not end well. In 2007, Gilchrist was removed from the board of directors of the Minuteman Project for accounting irregularities. In 2010, Civil Homeland Defense shut down.[15] And on July 11, 2016, its former leader, Simcox, was sentenced to twenty years in prison for child molestation.[16]

At the same time the Minuteman Project was generating so much publicity for itself, nativists in Congress stayed very busy. In December of 2005, for instance, a bill began making its way through the House of Representatives that, among other things, would have transformed all undocumented immigrants into felons. The bill—H.R. 4437—provoked a major public response from immigrants and supporters of immigrant rights. Beginning in March 2006 and lasting until May, hundreds of thousands of people demonstrated against the bill in cities across the country. But the demonstrators demanded more than just the defeat of this one bill. They wanted recognition of the fact that undocumented immigrants lived, worked, paid taxes, and raised families in the United States. For the demonstrators, undocumented immigrants were human beings who had earned the right to become Americans. But the nativists had a more dehumanizing view of undocumented immigrants as nothing more than an invading army. H.R. 4437 never made it through the Senate, but the nativism that inspired it is alive and well.

When people talk about "undocumented immigrants" (or "illegal immigrants"), it sounds as if immigrants who lack authorization to live in the United States are a distinct, neatly defined group of people—a group that could simply be skimmed from the surface of U.S. society and sent back to their homelands if the U.S. government just devoted enough money and personnel to the task. But reality is much more complicated than that. As of 2014, about two-thirds of adult undocumented immigrants had lived in the United States for at least ten years.[17] Roughly 3.9 million children enrolled in grades K–12 had at least one parent who was an undocumented immigrant. Moreover, 3.2 million of these children were native-born U.S. citizens. The other seven hundred twenty-five thousand

Latino Protesters Rally in Front of the U.S. Capitol Building in Washington, DC, in order to Reform Immigration Laws in the United States. April 10, 2013
IMAGE © ISTOCK.COM/COAST-TO-COAST

were undocumented immigrants themselves, although they may have spent most of their lives in the United States.[18] In other words, undocumented immigrants don't live apart from U.S. society; they are a part of it.

One of the more profound contradictions of undocumented immigration is that the escalating border-enforcement measures implemented since the early 1990s to keep undocumented immigrants out of the United States are, in fact, trapping them inside the country. As crossing the border becomes increasingly risky, and expensive, fewer undocumented migrants are going back home for visits. As a result, undocumented immigrants continue to send money back to family members still living in their hometowns, and perhaps even build houses in anticipation of their own eventual return once they've saved up enough money in the United States. Meanwhile, the children of immigrants grow up in the United States and have only tenuous ties to their parents' native land. With the passage of time, the parents themselves also come to regard the United States as home. Ironically, it is immigrants who have legal status, and can therefore travel freely across the border, who are most able to maintain social connections in both the United States and their home countries.[19]

Regardless of the degree to which undocumented immigrants put down roots in the United States, however, they can never fully integrate into U.S. society with the danger of deportation hanging over their heads. No matter how long they have lived and worked here, and no matter how many U.S.-born children they have raised, undocumented immigrants can be detained and deported at any time. Something as minor as driving a car with a broken tail light can trigger a chain of events leading from a stop by a local police officer to detention by U.S. Immigration and Customs Enforcement (ICE) officers and banishment from the United States. More cruel is the fact that undocumented immigrants brought to the United States as young children can meet the same fate. Even if they avoid deportation, they can never work legally in this country and cannot receive federal financial aid to attend college. Adding insult to injury, judges lack the authority to grant any sort of "relief" to even the most deserving person trapped in this predicament.

CHAPTER SIX

Warmer Welcomes

IF IMMIGRANTS ENCOUNTERED NOTHING BUT HATRED IN THE UNITED States, they probably would not stay for long, or they wouldn't come in the first place once they'd heard from those who'd gone before. But the fact is that immigrants also find warm welcomes when they come here. For instance, established immigrant communities in the United States provide a welcoming environment for newcomers. Immigrants who have just set foot in the country can settle into neighborhoods that are populated by people who not only hale from the same country, but often from the same village or extended family. This social network provides emotional support for the new arrival, as well as assistance in finding a job and a place to live.

Beyond the welcome they receive from their countrymen, immigrants are also accepted by many native-born Americans who have no real connection to the immigrant experience. Why? Because a great many understand the history of their country (and their own families) and realize that U.S. society has been built by successive waves of immigration over the course of centuries. At a more visceral level, many native-born Americans recognize that immigrants are human beings who are not threats simply because they speak unfamiliar languages, dress in unfamiliar clothes, and practice unfamiliar customs.

In addition to empathy and compassion, the welcome which some Americans give to immigrants also involves a fair amount of enlightened self-interest. In quite a few cities and towns across the United States, the native-born white population is growing old and shrinking fast. Birth rates are low and the few remaining young people are moving to more vibrant locales. This amounts to fewer workers, taxpayers, consumers, and entrepreneurs at a time when more and more elderly residents are aging into retirement and drawing on Social Security and Medicare. In a scenario such as this, immigrants are a life-saving transfusion that brings labor, money, and capital back into the local economy. Many local governments have recognized this critical fact and created "welcoming initiatives" that seek to draw immigrants to the area and ease their transition into local life.

Long before there were welcoming initiatives, would-be immigrants often judged how welcoming a particular U.S. town or city might be through the letters that they (or their relatives and friends) received from migrants already in the United States. These letters might seem like nothing more than private communications between members of a family divided by great distances, but they were much more than that. They were the most reliable source of information available on the economic and political conditions on the ground in particular U.S. communities. If you received a letter from your cousin saying that jobs were plentiful in New York and that most native-born Americans seemed tolerant of newcomers, you might be inclined to move to New York. But if the letter said that the job market had dried up and that immigrants were being blamed for the nation's economic misfortune, you would probably think twice about going. A good example of this dynamic can be found in the letters that German immigrants to the United States wrote to their families back home in the nineteenth century.

LETTERS HOME

More often than not, German immigrants who left their homeland and headed to the United States in the nineteenth century had relatives or friends waiting for them. In fact, it was probably from these relatives and friends that new immigrants received word when the time was right to pack up and head across the Atlantic to a new life. According to historians such as Walter D. Kamphoefner, the number of immigrants making the trip from Germany depended heavily on how good or bad the German and U.S. economies were doing.[1] Economic crises in Germany tended to drive more Germans out; economic booms in the United States drew more Germans in. And when Germans came, they settled heavily in states such as Wisconsin, Minnesota, Illinois, Nebraska, and Iowa—although the largest German population was always in New York City.

It would be difficult to overestimate the scale of the letter writing between the United State and Germany. Between 1820 and 1914, an estimated 250 to 300 million letters made their way to Germany from the United States. Of those, perhaps one hundred million were letters between individuals as opposed to business mail—although statistics of the time made no distinction between personal letters and business letters. Whatever the actual figure, the magnitude of the letter-writing enterprise is clear. And the information contained in those letters had a major impact on decisions made by individuals and families in Germany as to whether or not to immigrate to the United States—and, if so, when. Although there were other sources of information available at the time— newspaper accounts, travel guides, the promotional materials prepared by U.S. businesses looking for workers—none was as trusted as the personal letter from a family member, friend, or former neighbor.

Kamphoefner and his colleagues analyzed many of the available, surviving letters sent from the United States to Germany in the nineteenth century and noticed a number of patterns. To begin with, the writers of a great many of these letters were in some way answering that most common of questions among family and friends still living in Germany: should they come to the United States, too? Given the tremendous importance of this question, the letter writers seldom gave short replies. Rather, they presented reasons for and against emigrating from Germany, and then tended to emphasize that everyone had to make his or her own decision. The reason was simple: as much as German immigrants might have missed their relatives, they didn't want to encourage those relatives to come to the United States unless there was a very good chance that jobs and places to live were readily available. The writers of overly optimistic letters might find their homes filled with angry and resentful family members with no means of supporting themselves and nowhere else to live. This unsavory possibility kept most letter writers relatively honest about conditions on the ground in the United States, and inhibited any urges they might have felt to exaggerate how economically successful they were.

For people in Germany, these letters were the main sources of detailed information about life in the United States—and the writers of the letters knew this. And so the letters tended to be very comprehensive. There was much discussion of bread-and-butter subjects like job openings and wages in the United States (which many letter writers pointed out was strongly linked to how well one spoke English), as well as prices and the buying power of American money. There were also descriptions of what food, drink, and clothes were like in the United States, as well as what Americans themselves were like. American society was portrayed in mixed terms; neither uniformly gloomy nor uniformly rosy. U.S. politics usually appeared in the letters only in terms of who was running for president, what countries the United States was at war with, and how intense the xenophobic hostility of nativists was at the time. Oddly enough, descriptions of life in German American communities—the communities within which the letter writers usually lived—were sparse.

One surviving series of letters which exemplify this pattern are those written by Johann Pritzlaff, who was born in Germany on March 6, 1820, and made his living there as a shepherd. Johann's siblings included two brothers, August and Heinrich, and a sister, Elisabeth. Johann immigrated to the United States in 1839 as part of a Lutheran congregation looking for a chance to practice their religion without the government harassment to which they were being subjected in Germany at the time. Ultimately, they ended up founding a settlement outside of Milwaukee, Wisconsin—a rapidly growing town in which about one-third of all residents were German immigrants as of 1850 and 1860.

In a letter back home addressed to August, Johann states directly that he wants Heinrich, Elisabeth, and his mother to join him in the United States. He emphasizes that he is in a position to pay the travel costs, and that life in Wisconsin is better than in Germany. Heinrich's dream of becoming a carpenter would be readily realized in the States. Johann's work at a hardware store earns him enough money "to support a small family," so he could easily afford to have his mother and sister with him. He notes that officials in the United States don't act like the rulers in Germany and that the tax burden is not heavy. Johann also has a message for August's brother-in-law: being a tailor is one of the best jobs in the United States.

In another letter to August in 1847, Johann contrasts the scarcity of food in Europe with its "abundance" in the United States. He also answers a question that August had asked in a previous letter: how would he support himself if he joined Johann in Wisconsin. Johann replied that August, who was a teacher in Germany, could possibly set up a school in town given the large number of German children and the lack of good schoolteachers. In another letter written in 1850, Johann points to "terrible and tragic times" in Europe and says that August should immigrate to Wisconsin the following summer, if possible. He also notes that he may start a "small business" of his own. The historical record shows that he did just that, setting up his own hardware store, which became quite successful. And it is likely that August did eventually join him in Milwaukee.

Another illuminating collection of letters was written by six relatives who made the journey to the United States, one by one, over the course of ten years. The first, Anna, was the daughter of a largely destitute wine-growing family. She left Germany in 1848, at the height of a profound economic crisis brought on by crop failures and poor grape harvests. Upon arriving in New York she immediately found a job as a servant to a German American pharmacist. Soon after, she met her future husband, Franz, and—in the years that followed—they arranged for five more of her family members to follow in her footsteps.

Anna's first letter, from 1849, describes her luck at landing a job so quickly, although she points out that she would be earning twice as much if she knew English. She marveled at the size of New York City and its diversity of peoples and religions. And she ends by emphasizing that girls who immigrate to the United States can quickly find work as domestic servants, just as she did. In another letter from 1850, she tells her family that they would probably like it better in the United States than in Germany, although the decision to leave must be their own. And she says that soon she and her husband will have enough money to pay for Anna's brother, Daniel, to make the journey—although he would be well advised to find another profession, like tailor or shoemaker, rather than carpenter. In addition, she informs her relatives that learning English is hard, especially if one lives and works exclusively around other Germans, but that English comes much quicker if one works for Americans.

Later that year, Anna's husband, Franz, writes to her parents to explain that he'd lost his job recently and couldn't find another one for three weeks, which set them back financially. And he tells them that he and Anna don't think Daniel should come to the United States next given that he wouldn't be able to make any money right away. But if two of Anna's sisters came (both of whom were teenagers), they could quickly find work as servants. An 1851 letter makes clear that Anna and Franz have arranged for one of Anna's sisters (Barbara) to make the journey. A few months later, she arrived in New York after a twenty-six-day voyage at sea. Soon thereafter she had a job as a servant to English bakers.

As of 1852, the siblings' parents had decided not to emigrate. They kept their heads above water financially thanks to the money sent by their children in the United States. However, another brother and sister—Gottlieb and Katharina—did choose to leave. Barbara wrote that she would do her best to pay the cost of their journey. Daniel was told to continue waiting until all of his siblings had arrived in the United States, at which point they could help pay for him to come. Eventually, in 1857, he and his wife headed for New York.

A final example of the welcoming power inherent in letters concerns the correspondence of the Stille and Krumme families. Wilhelm Stille left the family farm behind in 1833, when emigration from Germany was just getting underway. In 1836 his nephew followed; and in 1837 so did his sister Wilhelmina and her fiancé Wilhelm Krumme. In the end, at least eleven members of the Stille family and twelve from the Krumme family left their homes before 1871. Emigration from the region where they lived in the province of Westphalia was driven in large part by economic stagnation. In fact, the population of the region declined by 6 percent (10 percent in some areas) between 1843 and 1858. Those hit the hardest were tenant farmers, which most (though not all) of the Stilles and Krummes were. They owned neither the land they lived on nor the house they lived in, and had been barely hanging on as is. When the economy tanked, their situation grew even more dire and emigration became the most viable option. And when they left, they tended to settle in rural areas of Ohio and Missouri. In fact, many of their relatives and friends eventually settled there as well. Wilhelm Krumme, however, landed in Wheeling, Virginia (which would become Wheeling, West Virginia, after 1863).

In an 1834 letter, written not long after he'd arrived in the United States, Wilhelm Stille almost immediately said that there was only one relative he would advise to join him: his nephew Rudolph. According to Wilhelm, Rudolph would do well as a cabinetmaker. He warns that his other relatives should stay put given that, in the area where Wilhelm lives, there were roughly eighty families, most of which live on the edge of destitution. He also notes that you have to work hard to get ahead in the United States and says that he can't tell his acquaintances whether to make the same journey he had made or to stay where they were in Germany. In the end, some people like it in the United States and some don't.

Wilhelm expressed a more optimistic tone in an 1836 letter. In response to a question from someone back home, he observed that there are churches in the area where he lives that conduct their services in German. And he points out that even though there are hardships associated with coming to the United States—such as learning English—immigrants eventually "get a feel for freedom," as well as an appreciation for the many crops that can be grown without the use of fertilizer, the low tax burden, and the ample and high quality food supply (at least when compared to Germany). Wilhelm also advises any of his relatives who have a significant amount of money saved up to buy land in the United States rather than in Germany because they'll get a much better deal. In a letter the following year, however, Wilhelm was more subdued. He informs his family that Rudolph, who did in fact come to the United States, died of dysentery. Wilhelm also mentions someone else who contracted smallpox during the voyage to the United States and subsequently died in a Baltimore hospital.

In an interesting contrast to her brother, Wilhemina complains repeatedly in letters from 1837–1839 about how expensive everything is in the United States and asks her family to send her a decent coat. She also advises her sister Elizabeth to not come to the United States; not only because of the high prices, but because Elizabeth is "too old" to work as a servant. Plus, there are plenty of Americans who don't mind price gouging Germans. However, her mood is markedly different in one letter from 1839—perhaps because she'd just given birth to a son. She says that she wouldn't want to live in Germany again under any circumstances. She also offers some advice to her sister Schallotha: if you can't marry well in Germany, come to the United States and bring all your money so you can buy a small place of your own.

Wilhemina died in 1843, probably from tuberculosis. Wilhelm Stille never ran a commercially successful farm and was always short on money, but he managed to get by with the help of his oldest son. Neither Wilhemina's death nor Wilhelm's precarious financial situation stopped other family members from coming to the United States. And they continued to receive the support—both emotional and material—of those relatives who had come before them.

WELCOMING INITIATIVES

Immigrants living in the United States today continue to exert enormous influence over family and friends back home who are trying to decide whether or not they too should leave the country of their birth. If a Mexican immigrant in Los Angeles tells his cousins that construction jobs are plentiful and that now would be a good time to cross the border, chances are that some of those cousins will soon be crossing the border. Conversely, if that immigrant reports that jobs are scarce or that worksite immigration raids across the country are making life in the United States risky, then his cousins might just stay put in Mexico. Of course, given the speed of communication in the digital era, most Mexicans will learn quickly when the U.S. job market starts drying up and the federal government begins rounding up undocumented immigrants. But on-the-ground reporting from a trusted source—whether by letter, phone call, text message, or email—still carries weight.

Aside from the social networks of family and community, there is another way in which immigrants today are sometimes made to feel more at home in a new country: initiatives by local governments explicitly designed to send a welcoming message to immigrants and assist them in integrating into U.S. society. Sociologist Manuel Pastor and his colleagues describe the relatively short history of such initiatives.[2] Many arose after Arizona passed S.B. 1070 in 2010, anti-immigrant legislation that spawned other immigrant-bashing state laws and local ordinances around the country. But many city governments sought to rise above this anti-immigrant tide by moving in the opposite direction. In fact, some cities adopted pro-immigrant measures that ran counter to the anti-immigrant vitriol emanating from the capitols of their own states. For instance, the Georgia state government mimicked Arizona by passing its own anti-immigrant law in 2011. Yet four years later, Atlanta opened an Office of Immigrant Affairs designed to welcome rather than attack immigrants, and to promote civil dialogue about immigration. Other cities—like Tucson, Nashville, and Charlotte— have done the same, also taking a stand against their state governments. At the time Pastor and his team were writing (at the end of 2015), there were twenty-six city offices for immigrant integration around the country, plus thirty-seven task forces, commissions, and welcoming initiatives devoted to the same cause.

Despite the importance of immigrant integration to communities from coast to coast, the federal government has rarely taken the lead in such matters. Once immigrants are admitted into the country legally, or arrive or remain without legal status, it is up to cities and towns to deal with them in a constructive way (helping them become part of U.S. society and the U.S. economy) or in a less-than-constructive way (either trying to ignore them or attacking them). In other words, localities must fill the vacuum left by federal inaction. Some do so with policies that are xenophobic, and some do so with policies that welcome newcomers. It's important to note that the Obama Administration did get the federal government involved in the business of integration with the creation in 2014 of the White House Task Force on New Americans, and in 2015, the Building Welcoming Communities Campaign (in conjunction with the nongovernmental organization Welcoming America). But when Donald Trump came to power in 2017, those initiatives were promptly scrapped.

According to Pastor and his fellow researchers, offices of immigrant integration that are housed within city government are the most effective type of initiatives designed to incorporate immigrants into the social fabric of the city. Task forces and commissions and other types of "welcoming" efforts are important too, but don't have the same kind of institutional clout as a dedicated office within the government bureaucracy. For instance, the Mayor's Office of Immigrant Affairs in New York City carries with it a long-term commitment to pro-integration efforts and has the power to make policy. In contrast, Tucson's Immigrant Task Force is a very useful forum for discussion of issues related to the immigrant community, but it can't implement new policies or reform existing ones.

Pastor's research indicates that successful offices of immigrant integration have a number of common elements. To begin with, they are actively and energetically championed by the mayor of the city—although, ultimately, they must become institutions distinct from the mayor. They also put out the welcome mat for immigrants and work at making the native-born population more receptive to newcomers. Successful integration offices build a broad consensus in favor of integration among community-based organizations, local businesses, service providers, and religious institutions. Learning how to do this effectively often requires drawing upon the technical expertise of organizations like Welcoming America. In addition, integration offices highlight the economic contributions of immigrants as workers, entrepreneurs, and taxpayers—a task which often requires the assistance of research organizations such as the Urban Institute. Some offices act as a resource center for immigrants as well, making city services more easily accessible to them. This might include facilitating access to English as a Second Language (ESL) classes, raising awareness of scams to defraud immigrants, and—for those immigrants who are eligible—providing assistance with applying for U.S. citizenship. Likewise, the offices promote civic engagement by immigrants through citizenship ceremonies, leadership training, and the organizing of diversity celebrations and other citywide events. Plus, city offices devoted to immigrants can coordinate the activities of other city agencies to make them more accessible to immigrants. In a related vein, they can work with local police to protect immigrants from federal attempts to transform the police into immigration-enforcement shock troops.

Immigrant integration is pursued by city governments for different reasons in different places. For some, it's primarily a matter of defusing conflicts between immigrants and a native-born population unaccustomed to their presence—in other words, combating xenophobia. This is the case in Atlanta, Nashville, Tucson, Houston, and Charlotte. For others, the focus is attracting immigrants to the city to compensate for a shrinking native-born population and to rekindle economic growth. This describes the situation in Pittsburgh and Dayton. Given that not all native-born residents are in favor of attracting immigrants, these cities have to deal with a fair amount of xenophobia as well. And there are those cities that have long been destinations for immigrants, but want to further assist immigrants in finding better jobs, earning higher incomes, buying homes, establishing businesses, mastering English, and—in the process—boosting the economy of the city as a whole. This includes New York, San Francisco, Chicago, and Los Angeles.

As an example of immigrant integration being fostered in a place not very accustomed to immigrants, consider Atlanta. The number of immigrants—particularly undocumented immigrants—in the Atlanta metropolitan area began to rise fast after 2000, driven in large part by the growing demand for workers to fill less-skilled jobs in the service sector of the economy. Given the hostility of the Georgia state government towards undocumented immigrants, it was up to the city to take a different path. In 2014, the mayor of Atlanta created the Welcoming Atlanta Working Group, which adopted a twenty-point plan to facilitate the integration and civic participation of new immigrant arrivals to the city. One recommendation of the working group was to create an Atlanta Office of Immigrant Affairs within the city government; a recommendation which became a reality in 2015. In part, the office encourages immigrants to come to Atlanta to set up businesses, buy homes, etc. But the office also works with other city agencies to adopt pro-immigrant policies. One especially critical pro-immigrant policy is that the Atlanta Police Department does not cooperate with U.S. Immigration and

Customs Enforcement (ICE) to track down and apprehend undocumented immigrants solely because of their immigration status—although other local police departments in Georgia do.

One city which is actively seeking out immigrants to build its workforce and tax base is Pittsburgh. As the quintessential "Rust Belt" city, Pittsburgh was devastated in the 1980s by the death of its manufacturing economy. Now, decades later, the city is still struggling to stay afloat demographically as its population declines. City leaders recognized that immigrants offered a solution. As of 2012, most of the immigrants in the city were Asian or white, and a great many were highly skilled. In addition, there has been an influx of refugees from Somalia, Bhutan, and Burma. The mayor of Pittsburgh sought to harness the economic power of immigrants by forming the Welcoming Pittsburgh initiative (which functions as an integration "office" in most respects). The initiative's strategic plan was developed in tandem with the city's economic growth plan, highlighting the degree to which immigration is viewed as a crucial economic resource. A major focus of Welcoming Pittsburgh is bridging the language gap between city services and the city's newest, non-English speaking residents.

San Francisco is the archetypal case study of integration initiatives within a city that has long been immigrant-heavy and immigrant-friendly. Just under one-third of the people living in the San Francisco metro area are immigrants. So it's not surprising that in 1997, the city government created the Immigrant Rights Commission (IRC), and in 2009, the Office of Civic Engagement and Immigrant Affairs (OCEIA). In 2008, the city offered municipal identification cards to undocumented immigrants. And in 2013 it adopted the Due Process for All ordinance which barred police from becoming de facto immigration-enforcement agents in the service of ICE. In other words, acceptance of immigrants and support for immigrant integration have long been central to the mission of the city government in San Francisco, and goes far beyond defusing tensions between immigrants and native-born residents. In fact, the OCEIA differs from the immigrant affairs offices in other cities in that it not only undertakes its own initiatives, but awards grants to non-profit groups devoted to similar work as well—although some non-profits are understandably uneasy about taking government money.

Pastor points out that welcoming initiatives and integration offices within city governments began to proliferate at a time when immigration in general and undocumented immigration in particular were in decline. In fact, the undocumented population as a whole shrank in the early years of the twenty-first century. Yet, at the same time, the public debate over immigration (especially of the undocumented variety) became much more polarized. The anti-immigrant side has grown more shrill in its warnings that the identity of the United States is threatened by the arrival of too many foreigners. They offer a pastiche of stereotypes, caricatures, and doomsday scenarios in which immigrant "invaders" are eroding the way of life so painstakingly constructed by native-born (white) Americans. Nativists labor under the misconception that to preserve the lives of natives they must destroy the lives of immigrants. But it doesn't have to be that way.

The pro-immigrant side has proven to be a bit more constructive—calling for the building of an infrastructure for immigrant integration. Some cities have tried to do this on a relatively small scale. The size of the effort notwithstanding, integration initiatives seek to harness the economic and cultural power of immigration in ways that benefit immigrants and natives alike.

PART 3

THE NEW ORDINARY

CHAPTER SEVEN

The Bottom Line

THE U.S. ECONOMY RELIES HEAVILY UPON IMMIGRANT WORKERS TO perform all sorts of jobs. Some immigrants pick crops, cut lawns, clean hotel rooms and offices, prepare and serve fast food, wash dishes in restaurants, and build homes. Others treat patients, conduct scientific research, design computers, create new software, and invent new technologies. Overall, there were 26.3 million immigrants in the U.S. labor force as of 2015, accounting for one out of every six workers in the country. But immigrants are a much larger share of the workforce in those jobs that don't require a high-school diploma, as well as those that require a graduate degree.[1]

However, workers are much more than the jobs they perform. Workers don't simply "fill" jobs; they also create them. Regardless of whether they are immigrants or native-born, undocumented or legal, all workers buy goods and services from U.S. businesses, or even start their own businesses, thereby sustaining other U.S. jobs. Plus, when these new workers/consumers show up in a particular area, the businesses that are already there often expand, and new businesses are created, in order to cater to all of these new customers. This process creates new jobs as well. On top of that, all of these workers and consumers and business owners pay taxes which flow into federal, state, and local treasuries, funding basic services and paying for the jobs of government employees.[2]

The point is that when nativists claim that immigrants must be stealing jobs from native-born workers, they are betraying their own economic ignorance. There is no fixed number of jobs just waiting to be taken. Workers are consumers who support businesses that employ other workers who pay taxes and sustain the jobs of other workers. When workers are let go, the ripple effect costs other people their jobs. And when new workers are hired, the ripple effect creates other jobs. It is a complex web of economic relationships that cannot be captured by a slogan or political sound bite. As a result, it all too often is left out of public debates about the ways in which immigration affects native-born workers and the U.S. economy as a whole.

THE BIG PICTURE

One of the most authoritative attempts to unravel the complexities of this topic is a 2017 report from the National Academies of Sciences, Engineering, and Medicine (NAS).[3] The report, edited by economists Francine Blau and Christopher Mackie, examines some of the most politically contentious issues in the public debate over U.S. immigration policy—such as whether immigration decreases or increases job opportunities and wages for native-born workers, and how immigration affects government revenue and expenditures. This is no small feat considering that immigration is just one factor among many that impact jobs, wages, and the fiscal balance sheet. Disentangling immigration from all the other economic forces at play is a tricky business. And the various studies which try to do so come to different conclusions depending on what methodology they use.

Nevertheless, the NAS report surveys the available literature on this topic and reaches a number of important conclusions. First of all, the NAS finds that, over the course of ten years or so, immigration has very little impact one way or another on the wages of native-born workers as a whole. There are two exceptions: the arrival of new immigrants can slightly lower the wages of immigrants who are already here, as well as the wages of the 8 percent of native-born workers who never finished high school.[4] The reason that immigration has such a small and limited effect on wages is that immigrants and native-born workers are not perfect substitutes for one another; for instance, they tend to differ in their job skills and their English-language abilities. All of which is to say that, more often than not, immigrants and natives perform different types of jobs and aren't in direct competition with each other. For this reason, immigration also has very little impact on employment among native-born workers. As more immigrants join the labor force, the number of jobs held by natives does not begin to decrease. Again, this is due to the fact that immigrants and natives cannot be swapped for one another like batteries—as well as the fact that the number of jobs in any economy is fluid.

The NAS report tackles another thorny topic: how much immigrants and their children pay in taxes versus how much they cost as measured by the value of the government services they utilize. This is an admittedly narrow focus that doesn't take into account the value of the work that immigrants perform, but it is a recurring subject of debate among policymakers and political commentators. According to the NAS, when viewed over the course of seventy-five years, immigrants generally come out on top at the federal level. This is because they come to the United States early in their working-age years and pay taxes for decades before they're even eligible for federal benefits like Social Security and Medicare (unless they are undocumented, in which case they are never eligible for federal benefits).

At the state and local level, however, immigrants end up using services worth more than what they pay in taxes. This is due not to the immigrants themselves, but their U.S.-born children. These children, just like the children of natives, are costly. They go through years of elementary and high school before they even start working and paying taxes. And so their education is counted as an expense incurred by their parents—an expense which the parents can't cover through their own tax payments. The irony is that the U.S.-born children of immigrants, once they're working, taxpaying adults, come out looking better on the balance sheet than either their parents or the rest of the native-born population.

Despite all of the emphasis on wages, employment levels, and tax revenue, the NAS report is quick to note that this sort of narrow focus obscures some of the broader economic benefits that flow from immigration. Such as the fact that the arrival of younger, working-age immigrants is allowing the United States to compensate for the graying of the workforce as the Baby Boomers enter their retirement years. Or that immigrants, and their children, aren't just workers, but consumers who help sustain key sectors of the U.S. economy like housing with their purchasing power. Plus, immigrants—particularly those who are highly educated—create businesses, make scientific discoveries, and design new technologies, all of which fuels economic growth and creates new jobs. In fact, some studies have found that the presence of high-skilled immigrants in the labor force may slightly improve the wages and job prospects of native-born Americans in general, be they more educated or less educated. Again, this is due in large measure to the fact that high-skilled immigrants tend to complement, rather than substitute for, the talents and abilities of the native-born.

A prime example of high-skilled immigrants creating jobs and adding value to the U.S. economy is the high-tech immigrant entrepreneurs of Silicon Valley—particularly those from India. Combining expertise in computers or engineering with business savvy, these entrepreneurs often succeed in creating dynamic companies that promote innovative ideas and hire workers in many countries, including the United States. Yet it should always be kept in mind that workers with PhDs aren't the only ones who play critical economic roles. There are, and have long been, plenty of immigrant workers with very little (if any) formal education who build and maintain the nation's essential infrastructure. In the nineteenth century, for example, Mexican workers laid the tracks that allowed trains to run throughout the Southwest of the United States.

THE *TRAQUEROS*

A defining historical moment for Mexicans who lived in the north of Mexico during the nineteenth century was the U.S.-Mexican War of 1846–1848. When Mexico lost more than half of its territory to the United States, numerous Mexicans suddenly found themselves living in a foreign society that lumped them in with other stigmatized and demonized minorities like American Indians and Africans—and treated them accordingly. As historian Jeffrey Marcos Garcilazo describes, U.S. victory in the war was widely attributed by Americans to the supposed racial superiority of Anglos over Mexicans, and as evidence of their God-given right to conquer whatever territory they regarded as essential to the progress of the nation.[5]

While this racist notion of progress meant different things to different Americans, there is little doubt that the opening of U.S. rail lines from coast to coast was near the top of everybody's list. Mexico (and Mexicans) were seen as obstacles to the expansion of the railroads—and the vast amount of trade which the railroads made possible—so the U.S. government took the lands it wanted by force. The Plains Indians who lived on these newly conquered western lands were also viewed as impediments to the advancement of the nation. The Indians saw the situation a bit differently and fought back against the expansion of the railroads through their land. Railroad crews were often supplied with guns in order to repel Indian attacks. In the end, however, the U.S. military quelled this armed rebellion by killing off or forcibly resettling the indigenous population.

The railroads were the archetypal Big Business in many respects. In 1880, there were four hundred thousand railroad workers in the country, compared to roughly three hundred thousand workers in textile mills and two hundred thirty thousand miners. By 1900, railroad workers numbered more than one million. As of 1890, there were ninety-three thousand miles of track representing an investment of $5.4 billion. A vital colonial function performed by the railroads was the mass movement of people into the Southwest. The Indian Territory between Kansas and Texas had a population of seven thousand in 1880, which—nine years later—had risen to one hundred ten thousand. Railroads also made possible the mining boom of the 1880s. In the Southwest at this time, copper was a highly sought after mineral due to its industrial uses. And railroads stimulated the growth of agriculture in the Southwest, bringing in the machinery needed for mechanized farming and hauling the produce to market.

Railroads not only tied distant western territories to the banking and industrial centers of power in the Northeast of the United States; they also extended into Mexico and connected them to the very same centers of power. There was considerable opposition at the time to the prospect of investment capital from the United States (and Britain) taking root in Mexico. After all, it had only been a couple of generations since the United States had seized and annexed half the territory belonging to its southern neighbor.

Between 1880 and 1900, railroad companies relied upon the labor of Mexican, Indian, Chinese, Japanese, European, and native-born workers. Typically, workers from the same part of the world were on the same work gangs—in part because they felt more comfortable with that arrangement. But from the point of view of railroad owners and managers, this had the added benefit of keeping workers divided. So when one group of workers went on strike to demand better pay or conditions, they were replaced by workers of a different ethnicity. The two groups of workers would then fight one another rather than form a united front against the railroad owners.

The anti-Chinese violence of the late 1870s and early 1880s (a fair amount of it perpetrated by non-Chinese railroad workers), and the Chinese Exclusion Act of 1882, resulted in a dwindling supply of Chinese railroad workers. And so the railroad companies turned to the ample supply of Mexicans to take their place. The hiring of Mexican railroad workers really began to take off in 1881 with the convergence of the American and Mexican railways in El Paso. Mexicans were presumed to be better able to handle the harsh conditions—especially the intense heat—that prevailed in much of the Southwest. And they would work for lower pay than either native-born whites or immigrants from Europe. This was something for which native-born whites could resent Mexicans, despite the fact that it was the railroad owners who profited from paying so little, not the Mexican workers. Although most of these workers were men, in some isolated locations Mexican women worked alongside their husbands—for half the pay.

Mexican railroad workers were known at the time as "common labor." That is, they were presumably unskilled workers performing raw physical labor in a job market that was low-paid, seasonal, and subject to wildly fluctuating demand depending on business conditions. Employers could hire or lay off large numbers of these workers with relative ease—or bring them in to replace striking workers. Yet many experienced Mexican workers possessed a wealth of specialized knowledge; as much as foremen and, sometimes, as much as engineers. Mexican workers were called *traqueros* because their main task was to lay down and replace railroad tracks (ties and rails). They also drove spikes into the ground, dug ditches, graded road beds, and performed many of the other backbreaking tasks that were, by any measure, the toughest—and most dangerous—jobs the railroad business had to offer. *Traqueros* suffered more injuries and deaths than any other segment of the railroad workforce. They were hit by trains and buried alive by cave-ins. They lost fingers and limbs. They broke bones.

For this work they earned about one dollar per day—compared, say, to the three dollars per day that an Irish immigrant working on the Union Pacific transcontinental railroad might earn. But Mexican *traqueros* also had in mind the fact that, back in Mexico, the same work would have garnered twenty-five cents per day. Moreover, track work allowed for circular migration to and from Mexico: a Mexican migrant could work in the United States until he had saved enough money to go back home to Mexico to buy land or build a small business, and then return to work on the U.S. side of the border again when necessary. But the railroads preferred to hire Mexicans who were new to the business because these "greenhorns" were less likely to protest poor working conditions or low pay. A significant (though unknown) number of *traqueros* walked off the job. Mexicans who turned their backs on the oppressiveness of the railroad industry often went on to better-paying jobs in meat-packing plants, steel mills, mines, or farms.

It is important to keep in mind that, although Mexicans comprised the biggest ethnic group working the tracks in the Southwest at one time, they were never the only workers on the tracks. There were also U.S.-born Spanish speakers from New Mexico (*Hispanos*) and Texas (*Tejanos*), as well as indigenous groups from the U.S. side of the border (Sioux, Navaho, Apache, Pueblo) and the Mexican side (Maya, Zapotec)—not to mention those that straddled the border (Yaqui). It is often impossible to distinguish among these various groups just from looking at the names on documents from that era.

The presence of track workers belonging to so many ethnic groups from both sides of the border, not to mention the fact that the railroads were laying tracks in Mexico as well as the United States, is an indication that the border was in many ways little more than a line on the map. The American Southwest and northern Mexico were a single region experiencing railroad-driven industrialization and commercial agriculture financed by the same economic powerhouses in the northeastern United States. To this day, numerous communities in that region are rooted in both countries, despite the efforts of the U.S. government to fortify and "harden" the U.S.-Mexico border.

The way in which railroads acquired workers evolved over time. In the early 1880s, the railroads hired Mexican workers directly and sent labor recruiters to the border or into Mexico to find new workers. By 1900, railroads had contracts with employment agencies that were responsible for recruiting, transporting, feeding, and housing the workers. Typically, the agencies paid the workers in "scrip" (scraps of paper) that was redeemable in the overpriced company store where workers had to buy their clothes, tools, and assorted other supplies—and in the overpriced company dining car where workers got their meals. Inevitably, the workers often ended up in debt rather than in possession of any actual money. By the end of the nineteenth century, many a *traquero* deserted his employer to escape this oppressive cycle of indebtedness.

Railroads also relied heavily upon word of mouth to acquire new workers from south of the border—with a current worker letting family members back home know that jobs were available, for instance. Some railroads made a point of providing workers with free pencils, stationary, and stamps to write to people back home and encourage them to come work particular lines of the railroad or sections of track. This sort of arrangement was a clever way to get around the banning of "contract labor" in 1885 by turning current workers into informal labor contractors who would provide future workers. One unintended consequence of this practice was the overcrowding of post offices. In Colton, California, for instance, the post office was jam-packed with *traqueros* and other Mexican workers on Sundays, much to the displeasure of Anglo customers.

Some railroads went to great lengths to make themselves appealing to migrant workers. The Santa Fe Railroad, among others, encouraged its employees to bring their families with them to live rent-free in an empty boxcar equipped with a wooden stove. Access was provided to a communal water faucet, outdoor toilets were available, and sometimes old railroad ties were stockpiled for use as firewood. Despite these amenities, conditions in the boxcar settlements where workers and their families lived were hard and squalid. Extremes of cold and heat, poor ventilation, vermin of various kinds, contagious diseases (smallpox, measles, influenza)—all were daily features of *traquero* life.

In exchange for their boxcar accommodations, workers were expected to be loyal—and to rebuff the advances of radical labor unions. Railroad officials were also looking to reinforce a patriarchal model of family life, with men providing for women and children who stayed at home. This dynamic was viewed by the officials as a way to Americanize the workers. Ultimately, underlying the entire theory of what a boxcar style of life could accomplish when it came to transforming the *traquero* mentality was the racist assumption that Mexicans were quite happy to live very meager lives of borderline destitution.

Anglos viewed Mexicans as docile and compliant, with child-like minds and impulsive dispositions. As a result, many Anglos believed that *traqueros* needed to be guided with a firm hand since they lacked the ability to learn things quickly on their own. There were some foremen and lower-level managers who actually respected *traquero* work habits and Mexican culture. In fact, there were Anglo foremen who married Mexican women and led a bicultural existence. But none of this was sufficient to compensate for the pervasiveness within Anglo society of racist stereotypes about Mexicans.

Some of these stereotypes were rather contradictory. For instance, Mexicans were considered childish and stupid, yet were lauded for the work they did when they were new to the job and to the United States. Apparently, from the perspective of management, things went downhill the more acculturated a Mexican became. According to one foreman of this era:

> "*The Mexican laborer's first year is the best part of his service for the railway. After he becomes Americanized he begins to reduce his work. After the Mexican gets so he can talk good English and smoke a pipe he is not of much use.*"[6]

The element of truth lurking in this racist caricature is that neophyte *traqueros* tended to work the hardest to impress their bosses. More experienced *traqueros* knew when it wasn't necessary to maintain a breakneck pace—and when to resist the demands of abusive foremen through work slowdowns or stoppages, or by walking off the job entirely. Organized strikes and union drives among *traqueros* were few and far between given that the *traqueros* were at the bottom of the food chain in the railroad industry and tended to work in very isolated areas far removed from major cities.

While *traqueros* may have been isolated and exploited, the fact remains that they and other Mexican workers played key roles in the birth of an industrial economy in the Southwest United States. Mexicans provided critical labor not only for railroads, but for the mining, ranching, farming, and timber industries of the region. The railroads were the arteries through which the life blood of the southwestern economy flowed, and the railroads would not have functioned without the labor of the *traqueros*. At that time in history, workers and raw materials and machinery could only get from one point to another via the railroads. The importance of the railroads peaked and waned, but one legacy of the *traquero* era had a more lasting effect: the boxcar settlements planted the seeds of many Mexican immigrant communities from El Paso to Chicago.

THE TECHNO-CAPITALISTS

Before World War II, northern California's Santa Clara Valley was best known for its walnuts, prunes, and apricots. But, as sociologist Monica Biradavolu tells it, the Great Depression killed off demand for its specialty crops and, by the mid-1940s, the orchards were disappearing and the local economy began a rapid transformation, turning from agriculture to manufacturing.[7] After the end of the war, the San Jose Chamber of Commerce sought to attract new industries to the area, and these efforts paid off. The valley became home to companies like Ford, Lockheed, IBM, Sylvania, and Raytheon. By the 1970s, the valley—which would become known as Silicon Valley—was home to hundreds of high-tech firms.

Although popular mythology often portrays the valley as home to impoverished geniuses who invented revolutionary new technologies in their garages, the truth is that the defense industry played a large role in the area's phenomenal growth. For instance, Hewlett-Packard—founded in 1938 and one of the quintessential small start-up success stories—grew rapidly thanks to military contracts. By the late 1980s, the valley ranked as the most defense-dependent community in the nation. At the dawn of the twenty-first century, Silicon Valley firms continued to make defense-related electronics and guided missiles.

Another big player in the growth of high-tech industry in the valley was Stanford University—or, more precisely, Federick Terman, an electrical engineer and administrator at Stanford who wanted to create a strong high-tech industry so that engineers graduating from Stanford would stay in the area. To kick the engineering programs up a notch, so that they would produce the most in-demand workers for the area's private industries, he sought—and received—millions of dollars in Defense Department contracts. Terman also worked to foster close relationships between the university and local technology companies. What Terman and the university offered was access to research and to well-educated students who might one day be highly qualified employees. One particularly bold move was turning eight thousand acres of university land into the Stanford Industrial Park—a move which physically tied the university to a number of the area's high-tech companies, such as GE, Sylvania, Lockheed Aerospace, and Zenith.

The culture of Silicon Valley's tech community is marked by a high degree of cooperation and openness, even among workers employed by firms that are competitors. This cooperative atmosphere goes a long way in explaining why so many tech workers leave their jobs with one company in order to found their own. The same dynamic is at work within the Indian immigrant community of Silicon Valley, which first appeared in the wake of the 1965 immigration reform that abolished quotas based on national origin. In keeping with the culture of the valley, Indian high-tech workers and entrepreneurs helped one another solve problems and run their businesses more efficiently. However,

Indian entrepreneurs have no problem establishing partnerships with non-Indians. Sun Microsystems, for example, was founded by one Indian immigrant and three non-Indians.

Despite this cooperation, Silicon Valley is not some perfect world of interethnic harmony. A survey conducted in the early 1990s found that two-thirds of Asian professionals in the valley believed they were shut out of managerial positions due to their race. The respondents attributed this not to racial prejudice per se, but to the operation of "good old boy" networks that didn't include any Asians. Hence, whiteness at the upper levels of many companies reproduced itself because white managers tended to select managers who were like them: white. This led quite a few Indian workers to go it alone by forming their own companies.

Despite the barriers to upward mobility, Indian scientists and engineers had long been drawn to the valley. This had much to do with events in India as well as the United States. After World War II, the Indian government embarked upon a very deliberate policy of creating a large homegrown workforce of scientists and engineers to fuel the nation's economic development. Since the Indian economy couldn't absorb all of the high-skilled workers being generated by the country's colleges and universities, many made their way to the United States to try their luck in the high-tech industries of Silicon Valley—frequently after earning graduate degrees in engineering or computer science from U.S. universities. In fact, the advent of the Indian government's high-tech policies coincided almost exactly with the rise of Silicon Valley as a hub of high-tech activity. The forces of both supply and demand were running strong when it came to the migration of Indian workers (and students) to the United States.

The nature of migration from India to the United States has changed over time. In the 1970s, highly educated scientists and engineers moved out of India to fill high-skilled jobs in the United States. At the time, experts viewed this as an example of "brain drain," in which India's best minds were drawn to better opportunities in the United States. During the 1990s, on the other hand, Indians with tech degrees were in growing demand for low-end coding jobs in the booming U.S. software industry. Hence, Indian migrants engaged in "body shopping"—basically renting

Silicon Valley Has Become a Prime Location for Highly Skilled Indian Tech Workers
IMAGE © ISTOCK.COM/YHELFMAN

themselves out on a short-term basis to U.S. software companies. This was the tech sector's equivalent of menial labor. Since that time, a new pattern has emerged: outsourcing. A wide range of information technology (IT) jobs are now performed in India for U.S.-based companies.

As more IT jobs have headed to India from the United States, a new type of migrant has emerged: the transnational entrepreneur. Indians who have worked in high-tech companies in Silicon Valley (and other U.S. high-tech hubs), and who are familiar with how business is done in India and the United States, are creating companies in both countries. These entrepreneurs live much of their lives in the United States and in India, frequently traveling back and forth between them. As one Indian entrepreneur put it:

> "I don't have a home anymore, or you could say, I have two homes. I split my time between India and the Valley. I have an office in the Valley and one in Bangalore—the one in Bangalore is just being set up, so I have to go there constantly. I am a citizen of the U.S. and am

waiting for the Indian government to change its laws to allow for
dual citizenship. . . . My son is in boarding school in India."[8]

These transnational entrepreneurs have split workplaces, split homes, and split families. In a related vein, the companies that they create don't make money, sustain jobs, or foster innovation in just one country. Like any multinational entity, they play economic roles in multiple countries—and not just the United States and India. Tibco Software, for instance, was founded in 1997 by an Indian immigrant, is headquartered in Palo Alto, and has multiple offices in the United States, Europe, and Asia. It's 1,500 employees are scattered around the globe.

Many transnational Indian entrepreneurs initially came to the United States at some point during the "brain drain" era of the 1960s through the 1980s. They often arrived as students, earned degrees in engineering or computer science from U.S. universities, and moved into well-paying white-collar jobs in the United States. Little thought was given to entrepreneurial risk-taking. At the time, being a professional with a secure income was the path that brought high social standing. Interaction with family members still in India was largely limited to the sending of remittances. In traditional Indian society, self-employment—entrepreneurship—was viewed as the domain of castes that specialized in trading. It was not something that middle-class families dabbled in. Nevertheless, during the 1990s, the entrepreneurial urge took hold in many of these formerly content professionals with stable jobs.

An example of the entrepreneurial evolution of an Indian high-tech professional is Anil. He came from a middle-class Indian family where studying incessantly for his engineering degree was his number one priority. After receiving his bachelor's in electrical engineering, he went on to earn a master's at a U.S. university. Degree in hand, he got a job with a wireless networking company in Massachusetts in the early 1980s, was eventually transferred to the company's Silicon Valley office in 1987, and rose to the rank of manager. Then, in 1994, a non-Indian colleague suggested they go into business for themselves. Since they could always fall back on well-paying professional jobs, it didn't seem like such a risky bet. In fact, there is a sort of revolving door for Indians in Silicon Valley, whereby they move back and forth between full-time salaried jobs and entrepreneurial ventures. Sometimes those ventures fail; sometimes they succeed and are sold for large profits.

But for Anil, there were also cultural obstacles to starting his own business. As he put it: "There was never any culture of business in my family."[9] He was raised to view "business families" as families that didn't care about education because everyone knew they would inherit the family business—so why bother going to college? And so Anil saw a big distinction between doing well professionally and going into business. Eventually, however, his perspective changed. He came to realize that being a high-tech entrepreneur in Silicon Valley is about more than just making money—a high degree of technical understanding is required, too. In other words, Anil saw that it is possible to make a profit using one's education and intellectual skills. In fact, for many Indian immigrants in Silicon Valley, this is a fundamental distinction: businesspeople are money-grubbers; entrepreneurs use their brains.

Beyond attitudes towards doing business, Indian high-tech entrepreneurs credit much of their success to their families. As one described it, "you shouldn't overlook the role of the wives of all of us entrepreneurs from India, the sacrifices they are willing to make, only Indian families provide that stability."[10] As this quote suggests, most—though not all—Indian entrepreneurs are male, and their wives generally play supportive roles, even if they themselves have well-paid professional jobs. Some families rely on the wife's income to pay the bills while the husband tries to get the business started.

Making the leap from high-tech professional to high-tech entrepreneur requires more than just family support—it requires networking, be it through relationships with colleagues and friends or participation in formal networking associations. For example, one Indian engineer in Silicon Valley who made the leap fairly early (in the late 1980s) was inspired by seeing his non-Indian colleagues leave their jobs and start their own companies. He broached the idea of doing the same in conversations with Indian friends and received little encouragement. But, one evening, during dinner with friends, he brought the subject up again and received a surprising response from a successful Indian cardiologist: "How much money would you need?"[11] So the engineer took a check from the cardiologist, poured in some of his own money, drew up a business plan and formed a company that took off. The next time he needed funding, he took a more formal route—he hired lawyers and went to a venture capital firm.

The companies launched by Indian entrepreneurs in Silicon Valley obviously yield economic benefits for the United States: jobs, tax revenue, technological innovation. But they also produce benefits for India. Entrepreneurs commonly set up subsidiaries in India, thereby creating jobs. Anil decided to locate his second offshore facility in his home city of Calcutta, even though it is not a high-tech hub overflowing with tech-savvy workers. Nevertheless, his company went on to employ 150 people in Calcutta. Indian entrepreneurs also make sizeable donations to charities within India, and to their Indian alma maters as well. The founder of Sycamore Networks, for instance, pledged $5 million every year for two full decades to his college: the Indian Institute of Technology in Madras.

At another level, though, the allegiance of many (if not most) of the Indian high-tech entrepreneurs is not with any particular nation, but to capitalism on a global scale. As one entrepreneur put it:

> "I am here because this is where I can run the best tech company in the world. . . . This is the environment for entrepreneurship, for venture capital funding. If I were into making toys, I would go to China. If I wanted to grow coffee, I would go to Brazil. . . . We are not just in India, we are all over Europe, Asia, Asia Pacific. It is important for people to realize that we do business all over the world, not just in India."[12]

This isn't to say that Indian entrepreneurs don't have strong sentimental and family attachments to India—they certainly do. But, as businessmen in a capitalist system that transcends any one country, they make decisions based on what is best for their business at a particular point in time. Fortunately for them, India became a good place to do high-tech business starting in the 1990s, when the economy was opened to global competition.

Today, high-tech Indian professionals and entrepreneurs have a number of options as to where they can settle or set up shop—Germany, Britain, Australia, and any number of other nations where high-tech workers are in short supply. They are not being driven out of their home country by dire economic circumstances or an absence of opportunities. Nor are they all being inexorably drawn to the United States because there is no alternative destination that is economically promising. They are weighing the pros and cons, both economic and social, and coming to a decision on the basis of what seems to be the best fit for them. Fortunately for the United States, many emigrants from India choose Silicon Valley. And, fortunately for India, many of those Indian immigrants open offices in Bangalore.

Indian (and Chinese) computer scientists and engineers first started coming to the United States in sizeable numbers in the 1990s because U.S. labor demand for their skills was high. It didn't take long until one-fourth of all new companies in Silicon Valley were founded by emigrants from either India or China. But the economic benefits which flow from these trends can't be taken for granted. The numbers of Indian workers and students coming to the United States dropped thanks to the harsher visa and border-enforcement policies implemented in the wake of 9/11—not to mention the scarcity of new jobs during (and for quite a while after) the recession of 2008 and 2009. Nevertheless, the fact that U.S. high-school students persistently rank below average in science and math compared to other developed countries means that demand for highly skilled professionals from abroad in unlikely to disappear anytime soon. The bottom line is that there are many variables in this equation and no way to accurately foretell what the role of Indian professionals in the U.S. economy will be in the decades to come.

CHAPTER EIGHT

Generation Gaps

PARENTS OFTEN LAMENT THE "DIFFERENT WORLD" IN WHICH THEIR children are growing up; a world full of obscene slang, baggy pants, and new technologies. For many immigrant parents, this chasm between the generations may be as wide as you could possibly get. Someone who leaves behind a rural village in El Salvador, settles in New York City, and raises a couple of American children is truly bridging the gap between two different social and cultural worlds. Or, more precisely, the children of these immigrants are themselves the bridge. They have one foot in the language, values, and customs of the old country and one foot in the language, values, and customs of the new country.

PARENTS AND CHILDREN

Roughly one out of every eight people in the United States is an immigrant. Nearly as many were born in this country, but have at least one parent who is an immigrant. What that means is that, on average, one-quarter of the U.S. population consists of individuals who have a direct connection to the immigrant experience. These numbers, which are amply documented by the National Academies of Sciences, Engineering, and Medicine (NAS) in a 2015 report, highlight the fact that it's not possible to neatly distinguish between immigrants and U.S. natives, given that so many natives would not exist were it not for their immigrant parents. In fact, it is impossible to accurately gauge the impact of immigration on U.S. society and the U.S. economy without also considering the native-born U.S.-citizen children whom immigrants bring into the world.[1]

There is no doubt that the children of immigrants integrate into U.S. society and become more like the native-born population as a whole and less like their parents. But this isn't always a good thing. For instance, immigrants tend to be healthier and to commit fewer crimes than either their children or the native-born population in general. Plus, the progress that the children of immigrants make in terms of jobs and wages when compared to their parents does not automatically translate into a fairy tale of upward mobility. The children of immigrants are just as vulnerable as anyone else to the divisions of class and race that fracture U.S. society, and a great many eventually find that their ladder for socioeconomic advancement isn't tall enough to reach the level of their ambitions.

Nevertheless, education is one arena in which the native-born children of immigrants make great strides. Most children of immigrants equal or surpass the rest of the native-born population in terms of how many years of schooling they complete. But there is a lot of variation among children of immigrants depending on how educated their parents are. Not surprisingly, immigrants with high-skilled jobs and advanced degrees (most of whom come from Asian countries) raise children who generally grow up to be the most educated. At the other end of the spectrum are the families of immigrants who hold less-skilled jobs, have very little formal education, and may not even have legal status (most of whom are from Mexico and Central American countries). While these children go on to complete significantly more school years than their parents, they still don't quite match the rest of the native-born population.

The children of immigrants also make substantial progress over their parents in terms of earning higher wages and climbing the occupational ladder to higher-status jobs. But, again, how far these children advance compared to the rest of the native-born population hinges to a large degree on where their parents fit into the socioeconomic hierarchy of the United States. Those parents who had a steeper climb because they had very little education, didn't know English, lacked legal status, or belonged to racial groups that are discriminated against do succeed in raising ambitious children. But these children, despite making enormous strides compared to their parents, don't catch up with the rest of the native-born population. It would actually be unrealistic to expect that amount of progress in only one generation given the realities of life in the United States which so many children of immigrants face: wages that have not kept up with inflation, growing income inequality, decaying public schools, and deeply ingrained racism.

The pattern among children of immigrants when it comes to learning English is much more clear-cut: most of them grow up bilingual, being fluent in both English and the mother tongue of their parents (assuming, of course, that the parents aren't native English-speakers to begin with). The grandchildren of immigrants, in turn, usually speak only English and haven't learned much of their grandparents' first language. While many nativists view the eventual death of the first language as a sign of linguistic progress, it is actually the children of immigrants who have the more impressive (and marketable) skill of bilingualism.

Integration into U.S. society certainly doesn't amount to progress when it comes to health or crime. On average, immigrants are less likely than the native-born to die from cardiovascular disease or cancer. They are less prone to obesity or chronic health conditions. They are also less likely to abuse alcohol or suffer from depression. It is not entirely certain why being a native-born American leads one to be less healthy, but it is likely that a high-fat diet and low-exercise lifestyle play a big part. In a similar fashion, the greater the number of immigrants living in an area, the lower the crime rate and the lower the level of violence. Among the native-born crime rates (and incarceration rates as well) tend to be higher. No one can say with certainty why immigrants are less likely to commit crimes and be behind bars than the native-born. But it may have something to do with the fact that immigrants are, by definition, risk takers who left behind their countries of birth to build a better life for themselves and their families in a foreign land. They are highly motivated to stay out of trouble, especially since stepping out of line (even if they are legally in the United States) can get them deported.[2]

PASSING TIME IN CALIFORNIA
When it comes to immigration, California is a window into the future of the United States, according to demographer Dowell Myers.[3] The state

was the number one destination of immigrants when the modern era of immigration began after 1965. Although it has since lost some of its luster as the favored home of newcomers from other countries, many of the earlier immigrants are still there—and they've had decades to integrate into U.S. society and the U.S. economy. Their children have had time to integrate as well, meaning that the economic and social progress of parents and children can be compared.

One measure of progress is the rate at which California's immigrants and their children make it through high school. This is one measure by which immigrants themselves change little no matter how long they have lived in the United States. Based on Census data from 2004–2005, the rate of high-school completion ranged from a little over one-third among immigrants who were recent arrivals (here less than ten years) to slightly more than two-fifths of those who had been here thirty or more years. This isn't very surprising since most of these immigrants came here as working adults who had little time to go back to school. Among their children who grew up in the United States, however, the rate of high-school completion was over three-fourths. The rate inched up to more than four-fifths among the grandchildren of immigrants.

A different pattern emerged when it came to proficiency in English. Predictably, immigrants grew steadily better at speaking English the longer they lived here. One-third of recent arrivals in California said they spoke the language "well" or "very well" as of 2004–2005—a figure which rose to nearly three-quarters of those who'd been here 30 years or more. Among the children and grandchildren of immigrants, however, close to 100 percent had mastered English, which is exactly what you would expect of someone who had grown up in this country.

Steady progress is not as immediately apparent when looking at the share of immigrants and their children living above the federally defined poverty line. The majority of immigrants in California were living above the poverty line in 2004–2005 no matter how little time they had lived here. And that share did increase with each passing decade in the United States. But the children of immigrants experienced a slight increase in their poverty rate compared to immigrants here thirty years or more. In contrast, the poverty rate among the grandchildren of immigrants declined. In short, integration does not translate automatically into upward mobility, especially for the children of immigrants who were drawn here by the availability of less-skilled, low-wage jobs.

A similar, structural barrier was evident when tracking rates of homeownership. Among immigrants in California, not even one-fifth of recent arrivals owned their own home in 2004–2005, but that rate soared to more than three-fifths of those here thirty years or more. Among the children and grandchildren of immigrants, however, the rate of home-ownership remained basically flat. Homeownership rates, like poverty rates, are not determined simply by one's drive to become "American."

Leaving aside economics, two other indicators of integration into U.S. society are U.S. citizenship and voting. Among California's immigrants, the share who had become U.S. citizens as of 2004–2005 rose steadily from one-twentieth for recent arrivals to just under three-fifths of those here thirty years or more. Naturally, the native-born children and grandchildren of immigrants were U.S. citizens. Similarly, the share of immigrants who were voters rose along with the share who had become citizens (you can't vote unless you're a citizen), and increased significantly among their children and grandchildren. Statistics on citizenship and voting should be interpreted with caution, though, given that millions of undocumented immigrants in the United States cannot, under current law, ever become U.S. citizens—or even Lawful Permanent Residents (LPRs)—no matter how much they may want to do so.

There are two important lessons to be learned from all of this data on education, English proficiency, homeownership, etc. First, and most obviously, the children and grandchildren of immigrants have distinct identities and should not be mistaken for their immigrant parents and grandparents—no matter how similar they may look at a superficial level. Second, it's easy to overlook the fact that immigrants integrate more and more into U.S. society the longer they are here if the majority of the immigrants literally just got here and are not yet integrated. In other words, if 80 percent of immigrants in your state arrived within the past ten years, you may not notice that the other 20 percent who have been here far longer succeeded in learning a fair amount of English, buying homes, etc.

NEW YORK MOSAIC

In the NAS study, as well as Dowell Myers' analysis, immigrants were neatly distinguished from their native-born children and each generation was analyzed separately. In real life, however, immigrant families are a bit more complicated than that. Take the children of immigrants who are brought by their parents to this country when they are young. They are, by definition, immigrants. But if they come of age in the United States, becoming friends with native-born kids at school, mastering both English and their native language, developing an "American" sense of identity, then they have much in common with those children of immigrants who were born here. In fact, some of their brothers and sisters might be native-born. For this reason, social scientists who study the children of immigrants sometimes examine both the native-born children (the second generation) and those immigrant children who came here before the age of thirteen (the so-called "1.5 generation").

One such study, by sociologist Philip Kasinitz and his colleagues, takes a detailed look at the children of immigrants (both second and 1.5 generation) living in the Greater New York area between 1998 and 2002.[4] Relying on one-on-one interviews and Census data, the study took place among a diverse array of immigrant communities: Dominicans, South Americans (from Colombia, Ecuador, and Peru), English-speaking West Indians (such as Jamaicans), Chinese, and Russian-speaking Jews (or just "Russians," for short). Plus, these immigrant groups were compared to three native-born groups: whites, blacks, and Puerto Ricans. The boundaries between the various groups were not set in stone given that quite a few children of immigrants had parents who belonged to different groups.

Kasinitz and company, like the authors of the NAS study, found that, on average, children of immigrants in New York ended up doing better than their parents by many economic and social measures. The children of Chinese and Russian immigrants did the best, which wasn't surprising considering that their parents tended to be better off than many of the immigrants from other groups. The children of immigrants whom U.S. society defines as black or Hispanic (like West Indians) had a tougher time in the face of racial discrimination, but still managed to climb higher than their parents. In the case of children of Dominican immigrants, racism combined with poverty, little education, and low English fluency among parents stacked the deck against them. Nevertheless, most of the children advanced significantly beyond the circumstances into which they were born.

There's more to the picture, of course; starting with differences among the groups in terms of their families and neighborhoods. New York's African Americans and Puerto Ricans were the most likely to grow up in families without fathers. African Americans grew up with the most siblings, even though, ironically, it was the parents of immigrants who often came from countries with high birth rates and big families. At the other end of the spectrum, children of Chinese and Russian immigrants were the most likely to have both parents in the family—plus additional adults (like aunts and uncles) who could help with child care or contribute to the family income. Children of South American and West Indian immigrants also had the benefit of extra adults in-house. African Americans, Puerto Ricans, and Dominicans usually didn't have extra adults, or even two parents. These families found themselves in the poorest neighborhoods. However, the Dominicans had fewer problems with crime than African Americans or Puerto Ricans—evidence of the fact that crime rates tend to be lower in communities with lots of immigrants.

When it came to education, nearly all the children of immigrants in New York achieved more than their parents had, although dropout rates remained high among the children of Dominicans. Nevertheless, the children of Dominicans and South Americans went further than the children of Puerto Ricans, while West Indians did better than African Americans, Russians came out ahead of whites, and Chinese did better than everyone else. The worst records of educational achievement occurred not among any of the immigrant groups, but among two native-born populations: African Americans and Puerto Ricans. In fact, Puerto Ricans were the most likely to drop out of high school, be held back a grade, and land in special education classes. Not coincidentally, they were the least likely to have college-educated parents.

But it wasn't simply the fault of less-educated parents that their children didn't realize their full potential. The fact is that African American and Puerto Rican children living in poverty-stricken neighborhoods of the city were funneled into the worst public schools and subjected to all manner of blatant racial discrimination by teachers and administrators (not to mention police). Only the children of Dominican parents experienced something close to this level of hostility because they had dark skin and came from bad parts of town. In contrast, Chinese families lived in better neighborhoods with better schools than African Americans, Puerto Ricans, or Dominicans. And because of the stereotype that the Chinese are a model minority who follow the rules and don't cause trouble, the children of Chinese immigrants were far more likely to be showered with advice and encouragement from their teachers, regardless of how educated their parents were. Plus, the Chinese community placed a high value on education and widely shared important information about specific schools and standardized tests with each other.

Once children of immigrants were done (or almost done) with school, they usually landed their first job through contacts made with the help of family or friends—like most New Yorkers. They went on to advance beyond their parents in terms of the jobs they held and wages they earned, although their parents were sometimes starting off near the bottom of the occupational ladder. In terms of earning power, children of Dominicans and South Americans did better than children of Puerto Ricans, West Indians did better than African Americans, and both Russians and Chinese came out even with whites. And while the parents' degree of poverty or level of education played a major role in shaping the futures of their children, the fact of being an immigrant's child wasn't, by itself, particularly relevant in determining the kinds of jobs they ultimately had. At any rate, fears that children of immigrants might become some sort of permanent underclass destined to poverty and low achievement proved to be unfounded. Even when the odds were against them, children of immigrants usually managed to better their situation.

It's notable that children of immigrants in New York usually stayed out of the industries and occupations in which their parents worked. If there was a family business, the children tried to stay away from that, too. Overall, children of immigrants were most likely to work in office support, the service sector, and retail sales. But the exact mix of occupations varied widely from group to group. Many children of Russian and

Chinese immigrants worked in occupations related to computers and finance. West Indians were frequently found in health care, education, and social work. A great many Dominicans (as well as native blacks and Puerto Ricans) were service workers.

As the prevalence of low-wage and low-status jobs among some children of immigrants in New York suggests, it would be a mistake to romanticize the lives of immigrants and their children, particularly those living in poverty-stricken neighborhoods where public schools barely function. Many children of immigrants might do better than their parents and still find themselves in low-wage, dead-end jobs. This is a fate they share with many working-class New Yorkers regardless of where they were born or what color their skin is. It has little to do with their potential and much to do with the extremely unequal distribution of wealth and power in U.S. society. All of which speaks to the fact that immigrants don't assimilate into some homogenous U.S. society. Rather, they assimilate into society at different points along the class and race hierarchy.

With so many obstacles in their path, how do children of immigrants manage to do better than their parents, even under dire circumstances? One simple yet frequently overlooked reason is that they often have parents with exceptional strength and ambition. In general, it's not the lazy or complacent people of the world who uproot themselves from their home country and journey hundreds or thousands of miles to a foreign country where, more often than not, they will have to learn a new language and deal with frequent hostility from the natives. The values and character attributes of the immigrant parents tend to rub off on their children. Even a father who is barely literate in his native-language can successfully convey to his daughter that getting an education is of paramount importance to one's future.

In addition, children of immigrants have unique opportunities to craft their own identities. In part, they belong to whatever ethnic community their parents belong to. They see themselves—and are seen by many outsiders—as Chinese or Jamaican or Dominican. But they also identify as Americans—however they choose to define that. This leaves them straddling two worlds, two sets of social networks, two sets of cultural values, which can—in the right combination—be an empowering source of drive and creativity. The children of immigrants who belong to racial minorities that have historically been exploited by native-born whites in the United States have more to rely upon than the history of their own subjugation; they also have a rich history of resistance to subjugation that pre-dates the civil rights era. Put differently, they are not destined for fatalism and despair just because their parents make minimum wage and can't speak English very well.

Related to this history of resistance was the extent to which African Americans and the children of West Indian immigrants were involved in New York politics. Both groups shared a long history of battling racial discrimination. And both voted at relatively high rates: children of West Indians were as likely to vote as native-born whites, while African Americans were more likely to vote than whites. The children of Russian and Chinese immigrants, on the other hand, who were better educated and better off financially, were the least politically engaged. Not surprisingly, most young people, regardless of what group they belonged to, were politically alienated and proclaimed their distrust of politicians in general. But it is no coincidence that the two groups with the most experience in waging political battles against racial discrimination were the most likely to take part in the formal political process.

Measuring how children of immigrants move beyond their parents in terms of education, occupation, and income is fairly straightforward. Measuring how well they assimilate into U.S. culture is much trickier. For one thing, U.S. culture—like U.S. society—is fragmented by class, race, gender, etc. A man with light skin, an advanced degree, a high-paying job, and a nice house in an upper middle-class suburb probably has a different idea of what it means to be an American than a woman with dark skin, a high-school diploma, a minimum-wage job, and a decrepit rental apartment in a poor neighborhood.

That said, there are some generalizations that can be made about the children of immigrants when it comes to their beliefs and attitudes. For instance, children of immigrants are much more likely than their parents to believe in the equality of men and women. They also tend to be expert in the use of English, don't have strong ties to their parents' home countries, don't mind marrying someone outside of their ethnic group, and are prone to borrowing religious beliefs from a variety of different faiths—both Eastern and Western. And they are proud of their bilingual and bicultural prowess—not embarrassed to speak the language of their parents' home country.

It's also important to keep in mind that U.S. culture has been shaped by centuries' worth of immigration from every continent. American cuisine, music, fashion, and holiday customs have been derived from other cultures as immigrants bearing those cultures have joined U.S. society and, over time, become Americans. Trying to neatly define what the native culture is that immigrants are assimilating into is ultimately an exercise in futility. If a Japanese American eats a taco from a fast-food place, is it a sign of assimilation? If a Mexican American does the same, is it resistance to assimilation? These are the kinds of mind games you can get into if you take the assimilation concept too seriously.

There is one aspect of integration into U.S. society that is much more serious than fast-food preferences: learning English. A seemingly endless stream of political debate is wrapped up in the question of whether and how quickly immigrants and their children are mastering the English language. Contrary to nativist rhetoric, the fact is that—predictably—immigrants learn more English the longer they are here, while their American-raised children are bilingual. By the third generation (the grandchildren of immigrants), English is usually the only language, with the grandparents' native language being lost. While the nativists might view the loss of the once-native language as a good sign, kids who are bilingual actually do better in school. Speaking only one language is not a virtue. It is a limitation.

CHAPTER NINE

New Identities

"IDENTITY" IS A VERY SLIPPERY CONCEPT. IT'S ONE THING TO MEASURE the educational attainment of immigrants from a particular country and compare that to the educational attainment of their U.S.-born children. It's quite another thing to determine when immigrants, or their children and grandchildren, qualify as culturally "American." Trying to sort that out involves coming to terms with two inescapable facts of life: no person, or group of people, stays the same from year to year and from decade to decade, and neither does the dominant or mainstream culture of a nation. The abstraction known today as "America" is vastly different than it was a century ago. And over the past one hundred years, immigrants and American culture have changed each other irrevocably. Foreign tastes and forms of expression become mainstream, and the descendants of immigrants become American.

As a case in point, consider the evolution of the bagel. As historian Donna Gabaccia tells the story, in the 1890s the bagel was a rather nondescript food item among eastern European Jews. Jewish bakers made them for Jewish customers and, at first, no one else had much interest in them. Then, in the mid-1920s, a Polish immigrant named Harry Lender set up a no-frills bakery in New Haven, Connecticut, that made bagels. But now, the non-Jewish neighbors of Jewish immigrants began to sample them as well and began to develop a taste for them. While home economists of the early twentieth century tried to convince everyone that being Americanized meant eating a New England diet, many residents of multiethnic cities preferred to sample the exotic selection of foods made by various immigrants living next door to them. And so, by the mid-1940s, the Lenders bakery employed six family members who busied themselves trying to keep up with bagel demand from the Russians, Italians, and Irish who had developed a fondness for bagels.[1]

In 1962, the Lenders went nationwide with frozen bagels for supermarkets. In 1984, Lenders was bought out by Kraft, which produced softer, sweeter bagels in a variety of flavors. Somewhere along the line, someone had the idea of slathering bagels with cream cheese—a thoroughly Quaker invention with no relation to the culture of Jews from eastern Europe. But by this point, the bagel was no longer a Jewish food; it was part of a multiethnic pastiche known as "New York deli." At this point, the bagel's historical trajectory came full circle, in a sense. In reaction to the Kraftification of the bagel, a specialty market developed for more authentic, old-fashioned bagels among discerning consumers who didn't want to settle for the Americanized version of a Jewish food item from eastern Europe.[2]

THE NEW "ASSIMILATION"

U.S. society has been created by different cultures from different parts of the world ever since Christopher Columbus happened upon a continent already inhabited by Native Americans. In short order, the Native Americans were joined at the bottom of the new social hierarchy by enslaved Africans. Over the centuries that followed, streams of immigrant workers from throughout Europe and Asia were added to the mix. Under those circumstances, the old-fashioned idea of "assimilation" is inaccurate, to say the least. Sociologists Richard Alba and Victor Nee emphasize that the original concept of assimilation was based on the assumption that minority groups—immigrant and native-born alike—can strive for nothing greater than the chance to shed their own beliefs and traditions in favor of a culture created by White Anglo-Saxon Protestants (WASPs). In other words, successful assimilation means that you are acting white enough to qualify as mainstream according to whatever white authority gets to set the standards of whiteness.[3]

The flip side of this belief in the inherent superiority of WASP culture is the assumption that embracing a (nonwhite) ethnic identity serves only to hold people back. Naturally, if you believe that WASP culture is superior, then holding on to a non-WASP culture is self-defeating. In the real world, though, immigrant communities derive strength from their sense of ethnic identity. The home community, where you can be with your own people and speak your own language, can be a kind of refuge from the rest of the world. It can also offer a way to get started in business when much of the larger society shuts you out. In the first half of the twentieth century, for instance, it was actually better to be Jewish or Italian if you wanted to get started in the garment business because the Jewish and Italian communities were where most of the professional connections could be found.

Since the old idea of assimilation was based on a totally unrealistic view of U.S. society that ignored history, what would a more reasonable view be? One alternative is to see the United States as home to a "composite culture" that includes the traditions and beliefs of many ethnic groups. This is different from the idea of "multiculturalism," which emphasizes the autonomy of different ethnic groups rather than the gradual bleeding together of their various cultural practices. From this perspective, assimilation takes place when the boundaries between ethnic groups begin to break down, and the members of one group start perceiving fewer distinctions between themselves and the members of another group. By this definition, assimilation is very much a two-way street and not simply a matter of the people with less power imitating people with more power.

Seen in this light, the American mainstream is and always has been in flux. New immigrant groups and ethnic communities—and their cultural practices—have gradually been mainstreamed to the point that native-born Americans often don't remember what used to be considered foreign. For example, relatively few Americans probably know that the decorated Christmas tree is, or was, a German custom—or that Germans used to be considered a dangerous foreign presence on U.S. soil. It is also unlikely that many Americans know that the southern Italians and the Irish were both commonly considered to be racially inferior to the British. The successful assimilation of all these groups is, in retrospect, obvious. And much of this assimilation occurred as the American cultural mainstream grew to encompass that which had previously been defined as marginal.

Assimilation has never been a swift and easy process. It takes a long time and spans generations; not just a few years in the life of an immigrant. It is often hard to see in ethnic communities consisting mostly of immigrant newcomers who don't have adult children. This is a lesson that nativists have yet to learn. For instance, a common refrain in nativist circles is that today's immigrants from Mexico and Central America just don't have the same drive to assimilate as the Italians, Irish, and eastern European Jews of centuries past. But that is far from true. Many Italian immigrants, for example, had no intention of staying in the United States for the rest of their lives. The aim was to save up some money and then go back to Italy, although that often never happened. And so quite a few Italian parents tried to keep their children insulated from American society (and American schools) out of fear that they would lose their Italian identities. Yet assimilation happened anyway because it is not a course of action that one consciously chooses. Individuals and families make decisions that are calculated to improve their lives at a particular point in time—where to live, where to work, who to marry. Over the course of many years, those decisions can bring immigrants and their children closer to the American mainstream, at the same time the American mainstream gradually moves closer to them as well.

The assimilation of Chinese and Japanese immigrants of the nineteenth and early twentieth centuries was in many ways far more difficult than for the Italians. Not only were new flows of immigrants from China and Japan cut off by law in 1882 and 1907, respectively, but those immigrants already here were barred from becoming U.S. citizens. Yet, despite the legal barriers and the extreme anti-Asian racism that was prevalent throughout the country, the segregation of Chinese and Japanese communities began to erode after World War II. The U.S.-born children and grandchildren of these early immigrants gradually moved into mainstream jobs and mainstream neighborhoods, and began to intermarry with members of other ethnic groups. The anti-Asian laws came off the books in the 1960s, although Asians still endure plenty of racism to this day.

One of the pivotal mechanisms by which assimilation occurred in the communities founded by European and Asian immigrants in the nineteenth century was mastery of English. It was the children of immigrants, though, not immigrants themselves, who tended to be fluent in English. And the grandchildren of immigrants usually knew only English and had lost the mother tongue of their grandparents. However, this doesn't mean that all sense of ethnic identity evaporated along with the language of the ancestral home. Ethnic identity and assimilation are not incompatible. It is possible to feel like an "Italian American" without putting up walls to the American mainstream. Besides, "Italian American" is a very "American" sense of identity that has relatively little to do with the social and cultural life of modern-day Italy.

Assimilation also involved breaking free of the socioeconomic constraints that all too often defined immigrant communities. In general, this meant that children and the grandchildren of immigrants managed to surpass their parents in terms of education, occupation, and income—bringing them closer to the white mainstream in the process. In the case of the Japanese, Chinese, and eastern European Jews, the descendants of immigrants actually climbed higher on the educational and occupational ladders than the average white American. Of course, such opportunities couldn't be seized until they actually became available, so it wasn't simply a matter of immigrants and their children trying "hard enough" to get ahead. And there was no one formula for success that could have applied to groups with such different histories.

The early European and Asian immigrant groups all tended to settle in particular locations: Germans in the Midwest, Italians along the Eastern Seaboard, Chinese and Japanese on the West Coast and in Hawaii. Their children and grandchildren, however, increasingly moved to new destinations, sometimes new parts of the country or sometimes just out of the cities and into the suburbs (in the case of many Japanese, out of the farming communities and into the suburbs). The descendants of the European immigrants have gone the farthest in this regard. This process of "residential assimilation" isn't complete for any of the early immigrant communities, but it is well underway. Yet it won't necessarily lead to the complete emptying out of all the old immigrant enclaves.

One of the most powerful signs of assimilation is intermarriage. When two people from different ethnic or racial groups choose to get married, it means that they no longer view the social boundary between them as insurmountable. It's an indication that a tipping point has been reached in mainstream society as to what qualifies as "normal." The descendants of the early European immigrants are more likely to be intermarried with other ethnic groups than not. Most people wouldn't even take notice of an Irish-German marriage, for instance. Intermarriage between the descendants of the early Asian immigrants and outside groups has also taken off since the middle of the twentieth century. In fact, some Japanese Americans worry that their community might eventually disappear because so many young adults of Japanese heritage are marrying non-Japanese and having "mixed" children.

None of this should be taken to mean that an ethnic group must in some way finish being assimilated before it qualifies as truly American (whatever that means). Nor does it suggest that having a sense of ethnic identity makes someone unassimilated. Some people have a sense of what might be termed "ethnicity-lite," for instance. They might eat "authentic" Italian food on the weekend, know a few phrases in Italian, and consciously identify themselves as Italian American. But that doesn't imply that they are resisting becoming part of the American mainstream. Assimilated does not necessarily mean homogenized.

At any rate, it's relatively easy to demonstrate assimilation in immigrant communities that were founded a century or more ago. Assimilation takes a few generations to become fully apparent, and the older immigrant communities contain many successive generations. But it's different in communities that didn't exist until after the 1960s. The now-adult children of immigrants can be observed in those newer communities, but the grandchildren are still too young to give many clues as to how assimilated they will ultimately become. The only group of more or less recent immigrants who do not present that problem are Mexicans, who have been settling without interruption in California and the southwestern states for at least a full century. In their case, taking a close look at the second and third generations is probably a good indication of where the community as a whole is headed with the passage of enough time.

In terms of language, it seems clear that new immigrant communities are making the transition to English. Even among Mexicans, who retain Spanish longer than other immigrant groups and hold on to their mother tongues, the transition to English is well underway among the children of these Mexican immigrants. But retaining Spanish is hardly a bad thing. It's also expected given that many Mexican communities are very large, not far from the U.S.-Mexico border, and fed by new immigration. By the fourth generation, English is usually the only language spoken at home. And it's not that proficiency in English is lagging; it's that bilingualism is persisting, which would seem to be an asset rather than a liability.

Measuring socioeconomic success from generation to generation in the newer immigrant communities is complicated, and not just because there are often too few generations on which to base a conclusion. To begin with, there are large numbers of high-skilled immigrants, mainly from Asian countries, who enter the U.S. labor market with advanced degrees, high salaries, and prestigious job titles. Not surprisingly, the children of these immigrants do quite well in terms of education, occupation, and income; doing better than native-born whites is not a very heavy lift for them. Then there are other immigrants, from Mexico and Central America in particular, who arrive with very little education and earn marginal wages at the bottom of the job ladder. Their children tend to go to school longer, get better jobs, and earn higher wages than they did, but—as far as can be told from the Mexican experience—educational attainment seems to stagnate for many in the third generation. Exactly why, and what happens beyond the third generation, is unclear.

When it comes to where they live and who they marry, the children and grandchildren of the new immigrants break through ethnic boundaries. As their socioeconomic fortunes rise, and English fluency becomes commonplace, members of the second and third generation are more likely to move out of urban ethnic neighborhoods and into suburban communities where native-born whites are the majority. Of course, there are well-to-do suburban ethnic neighborhoods, too, so the move into a majority-white part of town is not automatic. In a society divided by race, it's disappointing but hardly shocking to find that light-skinned Latinos have an easier time moving to a white area than dark-skinned Latinos. Intermarriage rates also rise from generation to generation, with Asians in particular embarking upon marriage with non-Asians more often than Latinos marry non-Latinos. Asians who marry outside the group usually marry whites; Latinos have a more diverse range of partners, no doubt related to the fact that Latinos are themselves racially diverse.

It's certainly a good sign that the American mainstream changes over time and has come to include formerly marginal groups of people such as Italians, Japanese, and Jews. But it would be a mistake to conclude from this that U.S. society is destined to become a postracial, egalitarian paradise. It is true that, at some point in the middle of the current century, non-Latino whites will become a "minority" in the sense of comprising less than half of the total population. But that doesn't mean that skin color will no longer matter. The definition of "race" is flexible, but the use of racial dividing lines has, so far, been a constant throughout the nation's history. And race is about more than just skin pigmentation or bone structure; it's also about who has power—and who does not.

CREATIVE TENSIONS

By its very nature, the immigrant experience involves a perpetual tension between old and new. Most immigrants must struggle to learn a new language, adapt to a new way of life, and coexist with strangers. Under those circumstances, says sociologist Charles Hirschman, it comes as no surprise that immigrants tend to seek solace in traditions, songs, and foods that are rooted in their homelands.[4] However, immigrants—and, to an even greater extent, their children—play a prodigious role in fueling American cultural, artistic, and scientific innovation. Perhaps because of the ways in which they've experienced life from the margins of mainstream U.S. society, immigrants and the children of immigrants are often open to new, nontraditional ways of thinking. The end result is that many quintessentially American forms of expression, not to mention new technologies and scientific theories, spring from the minds of people who are, at least in part, rooted in other societies.

A classic example of this from the 1890s is Antonín Dvořák, a Czech composer who came to New York for three years to direct the National Conservancy of Music. While U.S. classical music at the time was devoted almost entirely to imitating the most famous European composers, Dvořák was not so constrained. In composing his *New World* Symphony, he drew upon African American spirituals and Native American chants for a new kind of sound. Audiences loved his symphony, although he was derided by some critics for being a "negrophile." Unlike his critics, who were immersed in a heavily segregated society, Dvořák recognized that African American music not only qualified as real music, but was distinctly American, too.

Antonín Dvořák
MUSIC DIVISION, THE NEW YORK PUBLIC LIBRARY. "ANTONÍN DVOŘÁK" NEW YORK PUBLIC LIBRARY DIGITAL COLLECTIONS. ACCESSED DECEMBER 4, 2017. HTTP://DIGITALCOLLECTIONS. NYPL.ORG/ITEMS/510D47DD-D7A7 -A3D9-E040-E00A18064A99

Other examples abound. Rouben Mamoulian, for instance—who immigrated to New York from the Republic of Georgia after living and studying in Paris, Moscow, and London—became a highly acclaimed director. In 1927, he directed an all-black cast in a Broadway production of *Porgy*—declining to use white actors in blackface, as was so often done at that time. While many white directors wouldn't work with black actors, Mamoulian spent time in South Carolina and New York to get a better sense of what African American communities were really like. His status as an immigrant outsider no doubt predisposed him to move beyond stereotypes in portraying African American outsiders.

Director Rouben Mamoulian and Cast during Rehearsals for the Theater Guild Stage Production *Porgy and Bess*

BILLY ROSE THEATRE DIVISION, THE NEW YORK PUBLIC LIBRARY. "DIRECTOR ROUBEN MAMOULIAN AND CAST DURING REHEARSALS FOR THE THEATER GUILD STAGE PRODUCTION PORGY AND BESS" NEW YORK PUBLIC LIBRARY DIGITAL COLLECTIONS. ACCESSED DECEMBER 4, 2017. HTTP://DIGITAL COLLECTIONS.NYPL.ORG/ITEMS/716ADED7-023D-1A00-E040-E00A18066FE1

This isn't to say that all immigrants or children of immigrants are open-minded innovators, but the marginality of the immigrant experience does seem to fuel creative tension. The fact that immigrants and their children live in a world that is forever in between two societies and two languages provides them with ways of expressing ideas, emotions, and relationships that are exceptionally rich. This vantage point of looking in from the outside can serve as a potent catalyst for innovation in someone who has both raw talent and a high motivation to succeed. Children of immigrants in particular hear the stories of their parents, about how much perseverance and sacrifice was needed to get ahead in a strange new country, and they often take those stories to heart.

The successes of immigrants and their children are not limited to Broadway, nor are they confined to decades past. The native-born children of today's immigrants tend to do better at school than their peers and are more likely to go to college. The National Spelling Bee, the Intel Science Talent Search, and the United States Chess Federation are all dominated by immigrants and their native-born children. Given the extreme commitments of time and effort required of these endeavors, this means that life in more than a few immigrant families revolves around the study and practice sessions of the children.

The preeminence of immigrants in fostering creativity of the scientific variety is also very much apparent. Albert Einstein, a refugee physicist from Nazi-era Germany, is perhaps the most famous example. But he is far from alone. Immigrants account for roughly one-third of the U.S. scientists to win Nobel Prizes. Immigrants account for around one-quarter of all working scientists and engineers in the United States. And immigrants comprise the majority of students in U.S. universities who earn PhDs in mathematics, physics, and engineering. Immigrants are also overrepresented as members of the National Academy of Sciences, as founders of high-tech startup companies, as patent holders, and as authors of the most widely cited scientific papers.

Perhaps it goes without saying, but none of these facts is an indication that immigrants and the change they represent have been welcomed with open arms at any time during the nation's history. There is a strong strain of cultural conservatism within human beings in general; an urge to stick to those customs and institutions that are familiar. Many people don't particularly value innovation or diversity when it touches upon traditional ideas of what families and communities should look like and how they should act. In fact, one way in which so many members of immigrant families have succeeded is by going into business for themselves or trying their luck in new industries that are less bound by discriminatory traditions than the older, more established ones.

CREATING CULTURE

When the racially charged national quotas on immigration to the United States came tumbling down with the 1965 Hart-Cellar Act, sizeable numbers of migrants from India and elsewhere in South Asia (namely, Pakistan and Bangladesh) started to make their way here. They soon found themselves in a rather strange cultural milieu in which many white people, particularly those of the younger generation, professed a very romanticized admiration for Indian spirituality, but not necessarily a great admiration for the people who were actually migrating from India.[5]

Take, for instance, the near-rapture with which hippies greeted Indian sitar player Ravi Shankar during the June 1967 Monterey Pop Festival. Shankar played classical sitar and certainly didn't qualify as a cultural subversive in India. But U.S. hippies, in their quest to build an American "counterculture," selectively extracted elements of Indian (as well as Native American) culture—including the image and sound of Shankar himself. In certain ways, as described by American Studies scholars Rachel Rubin and Jeffrey Melnick, the hippy idealization of Shankar in particular and Indians in general qualified as a sort of "racist love" in which stereotypes about Indians as more spiritual and less materialistic than Westerners turned the people of India into a caricature. Paradoxically, many white people were looking to the East for spiritual and cultural inspiration at the same time as many Indians were looking to the West and migrating to the United States.

The hippies were trying to turn Indian music, religion, and fashion into symbols of a new relationship between the white youth of the United States and the nonwhite people around the world who so often bore the brunt of U.S. military force. This was hardly surprising given that, at the time, the wars raging in Vietnam, Cambodia, and Laos were on the minds of most Americans. But even a well-meaning stereotype is still a stereotype and is ultimately dehumanizing. However, the hippies of the 1960s did not invent these stereotypes. By the time the bands took the stage in Monterey, there was a U.S. tradition more than a century in the making of mythologizing "the East," or "the Orient," as a mystically powerful place populated by otherworldly people.

In 1893, for instance, Swami Vivekananda paid a visit to Chicago to give a speech at the World Parliament of Religions (which was associated with the World's Fair). The next year, he founded the Vedanta Society. Together with the popularity at the time of Indian art forms, Vivekananda and his Vedanta Society stirred up many years of debate about the meaning of Indian culture and Hinduism—as well as the ramifications of Asian immigration to the United States. Before long, fear of a "Hindu menace" was growing, as were rumblings of dissatisfaction that low-wage Punjabi Sikh immigrants working in the Pacific Northwest as agricultural laborers might be taking jobs from native-born workers. One insidious stereotype was the fake Swami who hypnotizes white women and persuades them to give him money and sex. Yet, at the same time these racist images were circulating, so was an alternative image of Hinduism as being inherently more spiritual than the crass materialism of Western societies. Nevertheless, in the United States, the tide began to turn decisively against Indians in 1907, with the anti-Hindu riot in Bellingham, Washington. By 1917, India was explicitly within the Asiatic "barred zone" of countries from which immigration to the United States was prohibited.

During the long wait for the revamping of immigration laws in 1965, there was one Indian man who made a major impact on at least some of the American population: Gandhi. Peace and civil rights leaders, including Martin Luther King, Jr., were inspired by Gandhi and his philosophy of nonviolent resistance to oppression. King was also impressed by the fact that Gandhi was influenced by the U.S.-born Henry David Thoreau, who had been influenced by Indian texts such as the Bhagavad Gita and the Upanishads. It was an intellectual chain that in some ways came full circle. Until the 1960s, Gandhi more than anyone else embodied for some Americans the romantic and fundamentally distorted notion that the cultural cure for the social ills of the West might be found in the East.

When the 1965 immigration law finally came to pass, and Indians began coming to the United States in large numbers, a contradiction arose. In contrast to the hippy image of India as a sort of countercultural Mecca, there was the reality that most of the new Indian immigrants were professionals and technicians who didn't quite conform to the hippy image of what an Indian should be. Hence the embrace of classical sitarist Shankar as the embodiment of India, as opposed to the Indian radiologists and engineers who were calling this country home. Shankar very deliberately embraced his role as both a musical and religious bridge between East and West. Shankar was helped greatly in this regard by the attention bestowed upon him by the uber rock band of the times, the Beatles—and guitarist George Harrison, in particular.

Shankar knew that he was playing a part, and he played it to the best of his ability. He was no amateur when it came to show business, having begun his career in the 1930s as part of a roaming dance troupe. By the time Monterey rolled around, he was very deliberate in how he marketed himself to a young, countercultural, American audience. Ironically, even though Eastern spirituality was portrayed as the antithesis of Western materialism, select pieces of India's culture were being peddled to the hippy demographic of the U.S. consumer market as a commodity—what Indian writer Gita Mehta termed "Karma Cola." But Shankar was not the only Indian to go on the "hippy tour" in the latter half of the 1960s. There was A. C. Swami Bhaktivedanta Prabhupada, who led Hare Krishna chants in New York and San Francisco; the Maharishi Mahesh Yogi (guru to the Beatles at one point); Swami Satchidananda, who would give the opening invocation at Woodstock. In fact, there was so much Indian-derived spirituality at the time that *Life* magazine designated 1968 "the Year of the Guru."

Of course, gurus weren't the only Indian import during the late 1960s and early 1970s. There were Nehru jackets adorned with Indian or psychedelic patterns. There were flowing robes and beads. There were colorful textile wall hangings. This obsession with the East was confusing because it represented such a wide range of motivations among those who partook of it. Some white Americans were looking for a new avenue for political protest or an alternative spirituality, while others viewed the crass commercialization of another culture as little more than a "hip" fashion statement or a chance to make some easy money. The ultimate irony in this trend was that an imitation version of Indian culture was being packaged and sold to white Americans who were largely oblivious to the growing number of actual Indians living in the United States. Americans got to play act being Indian, while most of the Indians—with all of their human complexities—remained invisible. And although some Indians sold Indian culture to white Americans for profit, most of the profiteers were themselves white Americans. It is well worth noting that, while Shankar was inspiring young Americans to turn East, he was being criticized in India for turning West by embracing the hippies and their market potential.

Indians may have had very little control over how their culture was packaged and sold to an American audience, but the same cannot be said for Jamaicans and their impact on popular music in the United States. Jamaica had been inundated with American culture since the 1950s, so when Jamaicans started migrating to New York after the 1965 Immigration Act, they were already well-versed in U.S. television shows, movies, and music. Yet, as Jamaicans, they brought with them to the United States a talent for "bricolage"—drawing on cultural scraps here and there and recombining them to produce something new. When applied to music, bricolage created new sounds from familiar beats.

A classic example of bricolage in action is the professional life of Clive Campbell (a.k.a. Kool Herc), who came to the United States in 1967 at the age of twelve and within a decade became a founding father of hip-hop music. Campbell, who lived in the Bronx, knew quite a bit about popular music before he set foot in New York. He knew that DJs extended a song by switching between two copies of the same record because people liked dancing to particular parts of the song. He understood that good DJs were quite creative in remaking old songs so that they sounded new. And he was very familiar with "toasting" in reggae music, which meant having a vocalist add rhymes to a music track.

However, Campbell quickly became aware that reggae was not going to appeal to most New Yorkers. So he applied Jamaican techniques to the American music he already knew so well. The end result was hip-hop.

But the circumstances that led a Jamaican immigrant to invent a form of American popular music went far beyond his own personal history. It also has much to do with the shifting relationship between Jamaica, on the one hand, and the United States and Great Britain, on the other. Jamaica was a British colony for nearly three centuries and didn't cut the last of its political ties with England until 1962. At that point, Jamaica fell into the economic and political orbit of the United States, which had long ago anointed itself the keeper of all nations in its own "backyard."

Jamaica's strongest economic selling point soon became tourism—offering the island to American travelers as if it were a perfectly preserved slice of nineteenth century history. But this fantasy didn't account for Jamaica's prime minister during the 1970s, Michael Manley, who was a socialist committed to advancing the cause of economic justice for poor Jamaicans. The U.S. government, viewing the politics of other nations through a Cold War lens, worked to undermine Manley's policies, with the aid of the international institutions it dominated (namely, the World Bank and the International Monetary Fund). As the 1980s progressed, Jamaica became a transshipment point for Colombian cocaine destined for the U.S. crack market, the government was mired in foreign debt, and many rural Jamaicans with zero prospects in the countryside headed to the cities—or onward to New York.

The migrant exodus from Jamaica was massive given the relatively small size of the island's population. In the 1980s, roughly 9 percent (two hundred thirteen thousand) of the island's inhabitants left for the United States—mainly New York. In the process, Jamaicans added a distinctive Caribbean flavor to New York culture. But many Jamaicans who stayed in Jamaica resented being abandoned by so many of their countrymen. Given the size of the Jamaican immigration to New York, it seems appropriate that one lyrical theme common among Jamaican musicians has been migration. More precisely, Jamaica is often construed as a place of exile among the African diaspora. This sets up a contradiction between the

Jamaican celebration of migration in song and the unease among so many Jamaicans with migration to New York. The unease frequently worked both ways, with native-born Americans terrified of the Jamaican "posses" of cocaine dealers who took up residence in the United States during the 1980s. Racially tinged U.S. media reports of depraved Jamaicans wreaking havoc on innocent Americans were commonplace throughout the decade.

Kool Herc exemplified something far more typically Jamaican than the cocaine business: the "cut-and-mix method" of creating culture. Before Kool Herc was on the scene, Jamaicans were taking ostensibly finished cultural products and putting them together in new ways to create something different. What Kool Herc did was to bring this Jamaican method to both American music fans and the DJs who played for them. And it was this method that instilled much Jamaican music of the late 1960s and 1970s with imagery and sounds from a typically American genre: the Western. Jamaican performers adopted cowboy names and used Western soundtracks to cast themselves—and their music—as Jamaican variants of the Wild West. It is more than a little ironic that impoverished Jamaican youth would watch American Westerns on the big screen, migrate to the United States, and make music that reinvented the Western for an American audience.

The post-1965 migrations to the United States from around the world sparked a great deal of anxiety among many native-born Americans about what the future held for the identity of their country. Seeing so many foreign faces and hearing so many foreign languages, some of the native-born pondered whether or not an alien invasion was occurring. And these worries translated into a steady stream of science fiction movies and television shows starting in the late 1980s and enduring into the early 2000s, all centered on the theme of alien invasion, albeit of the extraterrestrial variety and not the human kind. *Men in Black*, *Roswell*, *Independence Day*, *The X-Files*, *Alien Nation*, *The Arrival*—all featured aliens among us. Some of these movies and shows used thinly veiled references to migration and the U.S. experience with immigrants, including the supposed naiveté of those humans who took the invaders at their word when they said that they meant no harm.

An interesting aspect of the "alien invasion" strain of science fiction is that the outsiders—the aliens, the migrants—possess technology superior to homegrown human beings. This is totally the opposite of nativist stereotypes of immigrants in decades past, when they were commonly portrayed as backward and unsophisticated compared to native-born Americans. That changed somewhat with the rise of hip-hop, powered by Jamaicans skilled in the creative uses of audio technology. But the stereotype changed drastically with the rise of immigration from Asia—immigrants and children of immigrants who were often well-versed in the uses of computers and the internet. This was used to great cultural effect with the escalating number of Asian American "zines" (noncommercial, ostensibly amateur publications on the web, in print, or both).

This trend was kicked off in the late 2000s when a group of Asian Generation Xers resurrected as a zine an old monthly newsletter that had been released by UCLA students three decades before. The name of the zine stayed the same as the original newsletter: *Gidra*, which was an invading monster from a Japanese movie. One primary cultural function of the zines, which proliferated rapidly in the years after *Gidra* came on the scene, was to explore what it means—or can mean—to be an "Asian American." Which of the roughly 140 nationalities within Asia are encompassed by the term? All of them? And does "Asian American" include everyone of Asian descent, regardless of whether they are first generation or fourth generation? There were no clear-cut answers to these questions.

It is irony of epic proportions that the Asian American zine explosion depended on the internet, which was invented by the U.S. military, which conducted a war in Indochina (Vietnam, Cambodia, and Laos) that drove large numbers of displaced Asians to the United States. The basic idea of the internet came from the RAND Corporation, which envisioned a decentralized network of high-speed computers that could withstand the destruction of some of the computers because the remaining ones kept the system alive. Researchers soon discovered that the system was great for sending personal messages back and forth to each other, as well as instantly blasting out identical messages to anyone and everyone who subscribed to the network. These features would prove crucial to the development of the zine market.

Zines gained such a following among Asian Americans in part because Asians are the most plugged in to the internet of any ethnic group in the United States. Beyond that, however, is the fact that Asian culture became a crossover hit in the American mainstream at the same time the internet was taking off. Jackie Chan turned into a U.S. action star. Japanese animation was all the rage (Pokémon, Yu-Gi-Oh, the Powerpuff Girls). Karaoke transformed into entertainment for native-born whites. At the same time Asian became "cool," Asian Americans took to the internet to differentiate themselves from the very profitable U.S. corporate caricature of how Asians looked and acted. Moreover, zines gave Asian Americans a way to respond to their portrayal in commercial media.

A unique example of this frequently reflexive dialog in action was an Asian American pop culture zine called *Giant Robot* that launched in Los Angeles in 1994. It covered a wide range of topics during its lifetime, such as Asian junk food and haircuts to comedienne Margaret Cho's stand-up routine and a skateboarding visit to the camps where Japanese Americans were imprisoned during World War II. The zine was extremely popular and eventually became a glossy publication with all the trappings of a professional magazine: barcode, a subscription card with a credit card option, commercial advertisements. At this point, however, the duo who created the zine also started a new, stripped-down zine called *Robot Power* which was a spin-off of *Giant Robot*, but without gloss, color, or big advertisers. By losing the high production value of the first zine, its creators re-established their authenticity.

Zines gave young Asian Americans a chance to push back against the stereotype of Asian immigrants as the "model minority": hyper-polite geniuses who go to Ivy League schools, stay quiet, and live the American Dream. This is a highly condescending and constraining image that ignores the poverty and racism endured by many Asian immigrants, not to mention the fact that real Asians are real people with individual tastes and styles of expression. Plus, all too often, the supposedly model behavior of Asian Americans is held up as the polar opposite of the dysfunction which allegedly pervades the African American community. African Americans aren't very thrilled by this good-minority/bad-minority comparison, and neither are those young Asian Americans who identify with hip hop.

Zines produced by and for Asian American women are constantly taking on the popular image of the "geisha girl" or "China doll." It's telling that an internet search for generic phrases like "Asian women" or "Asian girls" turns up an alternate universe filled with pornographic films, photos, and websites—not to mention "dating" sites and mail-order bride services—designed to appeal to men in search of subservient and sexually submissive Asian females. One site, *Big Bad Chinese Mama*, took direct aim at these portrayals by posting photos of Asian and Asian American women deliberately trying to look as ugly as possible.

CONCLUSION

AT THE START OF THE TWENTY-FIRST CENTURY, THE TOPIC OF IMMI-gration became inextricably linked in the public consciousness to fear of terrorism. On September 11, 2001, a terrorist group claiming inspiration from Islam and calling itself "al-Qaeda" (the "base" or "foundation") launched attacks on New York and Washington, DC, targeting the World Trade Center and the Pentagon. Years later, a group with even more of a penchant for brutality—Islamic State (ISIS)—seized parts of Syria and Iraq. In addition to terrorizing the local populations within the territory it controlled, ISIS operatives, as well as ISIS admirers acting independently, carried out numerous shooting, bombing, and vehicle attacks against civilians worldwide. Attacks in Orlando, San Bernardino, and New York City, as well as Paris and Nice (France), received a great deal of media coverage in the United States. But far less attention was paid to mass casualty attacks in Yemen, Egypt, and Turkey.[1]

Events like these left many native-born Americans and Europeans fearful of all immigrants and refugees from predominantly Muslim countries. Anti-immigrant groups exploited the attacks, mounting public relations campaigns to convince the general public that the entire religion of Islam is synonymous with terrorism. These hate groups argued that the doors of the United States and Europe should be shut to any would-be immigrants or refugees coming from countries that are home to any terrorist group which claims to be ideologically rooted in Islam. The bitter irony in this line of reasoning is that so many Muslims have fled from ISIS, and that most of the group's victims have been Muslim.[2]

Sadly, far too many people in the United States are susceptible to the fear mongering of nativist hate groups, a reality that was exploited by Donald Trump in his campaign for president. Trump ran a campaign based heavily on the demonization of Muslims and Mexicans, and he did his best to pursue an anti-immigrant agenda shortly after taking up residence in the White House. Acting mainly through executive orders, he sought to kickstart construction of a wall along the entire U.S.-Mexico border, ban travelers from seven Muslim-majority countries (Libya, Syria, Iran, Iraq, Somalia, Yemen, and Sudan) from entering the United States, scale back refugee admissions, and ramp up deportations of any immigrants who were deportable for any reason. To justify such measures, Trump relied upon time-tested stereotypes of immigrants as dangerous criminals (or terrorists, in the case of Muslims), as well as job-stealing invaders. These were the same hollow stereotypes that the "Know-Nothings" used against Italians in the 1850s.

There was no evidence to back up those stereotypes in the nineteenth century, and there's no evidence now. Take a look three generations down the line from the initial formation of an immigrant community and you find that the boundary between what is "American" and what is "foreign" has become quite blurry. There is no shortage of hard data to demonstrate that fact. But racism doesn't have much to do with data or evidence, or even logic or reason—it's more about fear rooted in ignorance. And, ultimately, the only cure for ignorance is knowledge.

According to historian Patrick Manning, there are two tidbits of wisdom that are essential to making sense of migration—not only to the United States, but anywhere in the world. First comes the recognition that all human beings are basically the same, biologically speaking. The differences in skin color and body type which exist between different groups of people, and which are believed by so many to qualify as "racial" differences, are in fact trivial in a biological sense. The big differences between different groups of people are cultural, social, political, and economic—not genetic. Second, the real linchpins of human evolution have been the use of language and the drive to migrate not just from one geographical place to another, but from one human community to another. It is these social innovations that, together, have allowed humans to share ideas, to build on one another's ideas, and to transmit knowledge from one generation to the next.[3]

All of which is to say that migration is normal. It is not some unnatural, pathological occurrence. Throughout all of human history, people have been driven from their old homes by war or disaster, drawn to new lands by the prospect of a better future, or some combination thereof. This is one of the mechanisms by which human societies change over the course of centuries and millennia. Migration can and should be managed to the benefit of people in both sending and receiving countries. But it should not be feared.

NOTES

Introduction

1. Campbell Gibson and Kay Jung, *Historical Census Statistics on the Foreign-Born Population of the United States: 1850–2000*, Population Division Working Paper No. 81 (Washington, DC: U.S. Census Bureau, February 2006), table 1.

2. Complete country-of-origin data is not available for 1940 and 1950.

3. John Pitkin and Dowell Myers, *Projections of the U.S. Population, 2010–2040, by Immigrant Generation and Foreign-Born Duration in the U.S.* (Los Angeles: Population Dynamics Research Group, School of Policy, Planning, and Development, University of Southern California, October 2011).

Chapter 1: Living in Fear

1. United Nations High Commissioner for Refugees, *The 1951 Convention Relating to the Status of Refugees and Its 1967 Protocol* (September 2011), p. 3.

2. United Nations High Commissioner for Refugees, *Mid-Year Trends 2015* (December 2015), pp. 4, 6, 13.

3. Dirk Hoerder, *Cultures in Contact: World Migrations in the Second Millennium* (Durham, NC: Duke University Press, 2002), pp. 443–44.

4. Michael H. Fisher, *Migration: A World History* (New York: Oxford University Press, 2014), pp. 171–72.

5. Ibid.

6. Ibid.; Dirk Hoerder, *Cultures in Contact: World Migrations in the Second Millennium* (Durham, NC: Duke University Press, 2002), pp. 513–17.

7. David W. Haines, *Safe Haven? A History of Refugees in America* (Sterling, VA: Kumarian Press, 2010), pp. xi–xii.

8. Ibid., pp. 2–3.

9. Ibid., p. 143.

10. Ibid., p. 144; Roger Daniels, *Coming to America: A History of Immigration and Ethnicity in American Life, Second Edition* (New York: HarperCollins, 2002), pp. 337, 381–82.

11. Frances Fitzgerald, *Fire in the Lake: The Vietnamese and the Americans in Vietnam* (New York: Little, Brown, 1972), pp. 9–10, 375.

12. W. Courtland Robinson, *Terms of Refuge: The Indochinese Exodus and the International Response* (New York: Zed Books, 1999), p. 17.

13. Roger Daniels, *Coming to America: A History of Immigration and Ethnicity in American Life, Second Edition* (New York: HarperCollins, 2002), pp. 381–83; Walter LaFeber, *Inevitable Revolutions: The United States in Central America* (New York: W.W. Norton, 1984), pp. 314–15.

14. David W. Haines, *Safe Haven? A History of Refugees in America* (Sterling, VA: Kumarian Press, 2010), p. 6.

15. Refugee Act of 1980, Pub. L. No. 96-212, 94 Stat. 102.

16. This section is derived from John Doyle Klier, *Russians, Jews, and the Pogroms of 1881–1882* (New York: Cambridge University Press, 2011).

17. Ken Roth, "War in Iraq: Not a Humanitarian Intervention," in *Human Rights Watch World Report 2004: Human Rights and Armed Conflict* (New York: 2004), p. 13–36.

18. Ibid., p. 27.

19. Ibid., p. 13–36.

20. Ibid.

21. Iraq Body Count, "Civilian Deaths in 'Noble' Iraq Mission Pass 10,000," (February 7, 2004).

22. Lily Hamourtziadou, "Iraq: Wars and Casualties, 13 Years On," Iraq Body Count (March 19, 2016).

23. United Nations High Commissioner for Refugees, "Iraq Situation: UNHCR Flash Update" (November 15, 2016).

24. The rest of this section is derived from Madeline Otis Campbell, *Interpreters of Occupation: Gender and the Politics of Belonging in an Iraqi Refugee Network* (Syracuse, NY: Syracuse University Press, 2016).

Chapter 2: Hand to Mouth

1. This section is derived from Alejandro Portes and Rubén G. Rumbaut, *Immigrant America: A Portrait*, 4th ed. (Oakland: University of California Press, 2014), chap. 1; and Roger Daniels, *Coming to America: A History of Immigration and Ethnicity in American Life*, 2nd ed. (New York: HarperCollins, 2002), chaps. 7, 8, 9, 12, 16.

2. Alejandro Portes and Rubén G. Rumbaut, *Immigrant America: A Portrait*, 4th ed. (Oakland: University of California Press, 2014), chap. 1; and Roger Daniels, *Coming to America: A History of Immigration and Ethnicity in American Life*, 2nd ed. (New York: HarperCollins, 2002), chap. 16.

3. Jeffrey S. Passel and D'Vera Cohn, *Overall Number of U.S. Unauthorized Immigrants Holds Steady since 2009* (Washington, DC: Pew Hispanic Center, September 20, 2016), p. 4.

4. Douglas S. Massey, Jorge Durand, and Nolan J. Malone, *Beyond Smoke and Mirrors: Mexican Immigration in an Era of Economic Integration* (New York: Russell Sage Foundation, 2002), chap. 5.

5. Doris Meissner, et al., *Immigration Enforcement in the United States: The Rise of a Formidable Machinery* (Washington, DC: Migration Policy Institute, January 2013), p. 3.

6. Jeffrey S. Passel and D'Vera Cohn, *Size of U.S. Unauthorized Immigrant Workforce Stable after the Great Recession* (Washington, DC: Pew Research Center, November 3, 2016); and Jeffrey S. Passel and D'Vera Cohn, *Overall Number of U.S. Unauthorized*

Immigrants Holds Steady since 2009 (Washington, DC: Pew Research Center, September 20, 2016).

7. This section is derived from Jay P. Dolan, *The Irish Americans: A History* (New York: Bloomsbury Press, 2008), chap. 3; and James S. Donnelly, Jr., *The Great Irish Potato Famine* (Gloucestershire, England: Sutton Publishing, 2001).

8. Jay P. Dolan, *The Irish Americans: A History* (New York: Bloomsbury Press, 2008), p. 69.

9. Except where otherwise noted, this section comes from Ruth Gomberg-Muñoz, *Labor and Legality: An Ethnography of a Mexican Immigrant Network* (New York: Oxford University Press, 2011), especially chaps. 2 and 3.

10. Tara Brian and Frank Laczko, eds., *Fatal Journeys: Tracking Lives Lost during Migration* (Geneva, Switzerland: International Organization for Migration, 2014), p. 54.

Chapter 3: The Ladder of Success

1. Alejandro Portes and Rubén G. Rumbaut, *Immigrant America: A Portrait*, 4th ed. (Oakland: University of California Press, 2014), chap. 1; and Roger Daniels, *Coming to America: A History of Immigration and Ethnicity in American Life, Second Edition* (New York: HarperCollins, 2002), chaps. 7, 8, 9, 12, 16.

2. Alejandro Portes and Rubén G. Rumbaut, *Immigrant America: A Portrait*, 4th ed. (Oakland: University of California Press, 2014), ch. 1; and Roger Daniels, *Coming to America: A History of Immigration and Ethnicity in American Life, Second Edition* (New York: HarperCollins, 2002), chaps. 7, 8, 9, 12, 16.

3. The remainder of this section is drawn from Wayne A. Cornelius, Thomas J. Espenshade, and Idean Salehyan, eds., *The International Migration of the Highly Skilled: Demand, Supply, and Development Consequences in Sending and Receiving Countries* (San Diego: Center for Comparative Immigration Studies, University of California, San Diego, 2001), chaps. 1 and 2.

4. This section is derived from Bruce Levine, *The Spirit of 1848: German Immigrants, Labor Conflict, and the Coming of the Civil War* (Chicago: University of Illinois Press, 1992), particularly the introduction and chapters 1–3.

5. This section is derived from Paula Chakravartty, "The Emigration of High-Skilled Indian Workers to the United States: Flexible Citizenship and India's Information Economy," in Wayne A. Cornelius, Thomas J. Espenshade, and Idean Salehyan, eds., *The International Migration of the Highly Skilled: Demand, Supply, and Development Consequences in Sending and Receiving Countries* (San Diego: Center for Comparative Immigration Studies, University of California, San Diego, 2001), pp. 325–49; and Roli Varma, *Harbingers of Global Change: India's Techno-Immigrants in the United States* (Lanham, MD: Lexington Books, 2006), chaps. 1–4, 6.

6. Paula Chakravartty, "The Emigration of High-Skilled Indian Workers to the United States: Flexible Citizenship and India's Information Economy," in Wayne A. Cornelius, Thomas J. Espenshade, and Idean Salehyan, eds., *The International Migration of the Highly Skilled: Demand, Supply, and Development Consequences in Sending and Receiving Countries* (San Diego: Center for Comparative Immigration Studies, University of California, San Diego, 2001), pp. 325–49.

Chapter 4: Pieces of Paper

1. U.S. Department of Homeland Security, *2015 Yearbook of Immigration Statistics* (2016), table 41.

2. This section has been extracted from Daniel Kanstroom, *Deportation Nation: Outsiders in American History* (Cambridge, MA: Harvard University Press, 2007); and Mae M. Ngai, *Impossible Subjects: Illegal Aliens and the Making of Modern America* (Princeton, NJ: Princeton University Press, 2004).

3. Mae M. Ngai, *Impossible Subjects: Illegal Aliens and the Making of Modern America* (Princeton, NJ: Princeton University Press, 2004), p. 1.

4. This section is drawn from Erika Lee, *The Making of Asian America: A History* (New York: Simon & Schuster, 2015), chap. 9; and Erika Lee, *At America's Gates: Chinese Immigration during the Exclusion Era, 1882–1943* (Chapel Hill: University of North Carolina Press, 2003).

5. Dr. Q's life is detailed in Alfredo Quiñones-Hinojosa (with Mim Eichler Rivas), *Becoming Dr. Q: My Journey from Migrant Farm Worker to Brain Surgeon* (Oakland: University of California Press, 2012).

Chapter 5: Fearing the Unknown

1. Unless otherwise indicated, this section has been synthesized from Daniel J. Tichenor, *Dividing Lines: The Politics of Immigration Control in America* (Princeton, NJ: Princeton University Press, 2002); and Peter Schrag, *Not Fit for Our Society: Immigration and Nativism in America* (Oakland: University of California Press, 2011).

2. See, for instance, Mark Krikorian, *The New Case Against Immigration: Both Legal and Illegal* (New York: Penguin Group, 2008).

3. Manuel Roig-Franzia, "Mark Krikorian: The Provocateur Standing in the Way of Immigration Reform," *Washington Post*, June 17, 2013.

4. Daniel J. Tichenor, *Dividing Lines: The Politics of Immigration Control in America* (Princeton, NJ: Princeton University Press, 2002), p. 89.

5. Daniel J. Tichenor, *Dividing Lines: The Politics of Immigration Control in America* (Princeton, NJ: Princeton University Press, 2002), pp. 90–91.

6. U.S. Congress, *Report of the Joint Special Committee to Investigate Chinese Immigration*, February 27, 1877.

7. Douglas S. Massey, Jorge Durand, and Nolan J. Malone, *Beyond Smoke and Mirrors: Mexican Immigration in an Era of Economic Integration* (New York: Russell Sage Foundation, 2002).

8. Jeffrey Passel, D'Vera Cohn, and Ana Gonzalez-Barrera, *Population Decline of Unauthorized Immigrants Stalls, May Have Reversed* (Washington, DC: Pew Research Center, September 23, 2013), p. 9.

9. Except where otherwise noted, this section is drawn from Salvatore J. LaGumina, *WOP!: A Documentary History of Anti-Italian Discrimination in the United States* (San Francisco, CA: Straight Arrow Books, 1973), chaps. 1–4.

10. The newspaper stories from the 19th century quoted in this section were reproduced in Salvatore J. LaGumina, *WOP!: A Documentary History of Anti-Italian Discrimination in the United States* (San Francisco, CA: Straight Arrow Books, 1973).

11. Henry Cabot Lodge, "Lynch Law and Unrestricted Immigration," *North American Review* 152, no. 414 (May 1891): 602, 608–10.

12. Jerre Mangione and Ben Morreale, *La Storia: Five Centuries of the Italian American Experience* (New York: HarperCollins, 1992), p. 201.

13. Except where otherwise noted, the information in this section comes from Leo R. Chavez, *The Latino Threat: Constructing Immigrants, Citizens, and the Nation* (Stanford, CA: Stanford University Press, 2008).

14. These quotes from Huntington, which are cited in Chavez's book, are taken from Samuel P. Huntington, "The Hispanic Challenge," *Foreign Policy* (March–April 2004), pp. 30, 32, 42.

15. Sonia Scherr, "Top Minuteman Group Announces Breakup," *Intelligence Report* (Summer 2010).

16. Megan Cassidy, "Ex-Minuteman Chris Simcox Sentenced to 19.5 Years in Child Sex-Abuse Case," *Arizona Republic* (July 11, 2016).

17. Jens Manuel Krogstad, Jeffrey S. Passel, and D'Vera Cohn, "5 Facts about Illegal Immigration in the U.S." (Washington, DC: Pew Research Center, November 3, 2016).

18. Jeffrey S. Passel and D'Vera Cohn, "Children of Unauthorized Immigrants Represent Rising Share of K–12 Students" (Washington, DC: Pew Research Center, November 17, 2016).

19. Douglas S. Massey, Jorge Durand, and Nolan J. Malone, *Beyond Smoke and Mirrors: Mexican Immigration in an Era of Economic Integration* (New York: Russell Sage Foundation, 2002), pp. 128–33.

Chapter 6: Warmer Welcomes

1. This section is derived from Walter D. Kamphoefner, Wolfgang Helbich, and Ulrike Sommer, eds., *News from the Land of Freedom: German Immigrants Write Home* (Ithaca, NY: Cornell University Press, 1991), introduction, chaps. 1, 9, 18.

2. This section is derived from Manuel Pastor, Rhonda Ortiz, and Els de Graau, *Opening Minds, Opening Doors, Opening Communities: Cities Leading for Immigrant Integration* (Center for the Study of Immigrant Integration at the University of Southern California, Americas Society/Council of the Americas, and Welcoming America, December 15, 2015).

Chapter 7: The Bottom Line

1. Bureau of Labor Statistics, U.S. Department of Labor, "News Release—Foreign-Born Workers: Labor Force Characteristics—2015" (May 19, 2016).

2. See Giovanni Peri, "The Effect of Immigrants on U.S. Employment and Productivity," *FRBSF Economic Letter* 2010-26 (San Francisco, CA: Federal Reserve Bank of San Francisco, August 30, 2010); Heidi Shierholz, *Immigration and Wages: Methodological Advancements Confirm Modest Gains for Native Workers* (Washington, DC: Economic Policy Institute, February 4, 2010).

3. Except where otherwise noted, this section is based on Francine D. Blau and Christopher Mackie, eds., *The Economic and Fiscal Consequences of Immigration* (Washington, DC: National Academies Press, 2017), summary, chaps. 1, 5.

4. Camille L. Ryan and Kurt Bauman, *Educational Attainment in the United States: 2015* (Washington, DC: U.S. Census Bureau, March 2016).

5. This section is derived from Jeffrey Marcos Garcilazo, *Traqueros: Mexican Railroad Workers in the United States, 1870 to 1930* (Denton: University of North Texas Press, 2012).

6. Jeffrey Marcos Garcilazo, *Traqueros: Mexican Railroad Workers in the United States, 1870 to 1930* (Denton: University of North Texas Press, 2012), p. 70.

7. This section is derived from Monica R. Biradavolu, *Indian Entrepreneurs in Silicon Valley: The Making of a Transnational Techno-Capitalist Class* (Amherst, NY: Cambria Press, 2008).

8. Quoted in Monica R. Biradavolu, *Indian Entrepreneurs in Silicon Valley: The Making of a Transnational Techno-Capitalist Class* (Amherst, NY: Cambria Press, 2008), p. 103.

9. Ibid., pp. 127–28.

10. Ibid., p. 134.

11. Ibid., p. 139.

12. Ibid., p. 153.

Chapter 8: Generation Gaps

1. This section is drawn from Mary C. Waters and Marisa Gerstein Pineau, eds., *The Integration of Immigrants into American Society* (Washington, DC: National Academies Press, 2015), chaps. 6, 7, 9.

2. Walter A. Ewing, Daniel E. Martínez, and Rubén G. Rumbaut, *The Criminalization of Immigration in the United States* (Washington, DC: American Immigration Council, July 2015).

3. This section is drawn from Dowell Myers, *Immigrants and Boomers: Forging a New Social Contract for the Future of America* (New York: Russell Sage Foundation, 2007), introduction, chaps. 5, 6.

4. This section is derived from Philip Kasinitz, Mary C. Waters, John H. Mollenkopf, and Jennifer Holdaway, *Inheriting the City: The Children of Immigrants Come of Age* (Cambridge, MA: Harvard University Press, 2008).

Chapter 9: New Identities

1. Donna R. Gabaccia, *We Are What We Eat: Ethnic Food and the Making of Americans* (Cambridge, MA: Harvard University Press, 2000), introduction.

2. Ibid.

3. This section is derived from Richard Alba and Victor Nee, *Remaking the American Mainstream: Assimilation and Contemporary Immigration* (Cambridge, MA: Harvard University Press, 2003), chaps. 1, 3, 6, 7.

4. The information in this section comes from Charles Hirschman, "The Contributions of Immigrants to American Culture," *Daedalus* 142, no. 3 (Summer 2013): 26–47.

5. This section is derived from Rachel Rubin and Jeffrey Melnick, *Immigration and American Popular Culture: An Introduction* (New York: New York University Press, 2007), chaps. 4, 5, and 6.

Conclusion

1. Cameron Glenn, "Timeline: Rise and Spread of the Islamic State" (Washington, DC: Wilson Center, July 5, 2016).

2. Peter Bouckaert, "Syrian Refugees Are Not the Problem," *Foreign Policy* (November 18, 2015).

3. Michael H. Fisher, *Migration: A World History* (New York: Oxford University Press, 2014), pp. 1–2, 57–58.

INDEX

ABOUT THE AUTHOR

Walter A. Ewing is senior researcher at the American Immigration Council, a nonprofit in Washington, DC, that is devoted to the advancement of U.S. immigration policies that are both practical and humane. In the course of his fifteen years at the Council, Walter has studied and written about the impact of immigration on the U.S. economy and U.S. workers, the relationship (or lack thereof) between immigration and crime, the ineffectiveness and inefficiency of U.S. border-enforcement policies, and the faulty logic of the pseudo-scientific research disseminated by anti-immigrant organizations.

Prior to his time at the Council, Walter spent two years as an immigration policy analyst for the U.S. Conference of Catholic Bishops and two years as a program director at the U.S. Committee for Immigrants and Refugees, also located in Washington, DC. Walter has a PhD in anthropology from the City University of New York Graduate Center.

About the Author(s)